2002

Things To Do On A

DATE

2002

Things To Do On A

DATE

From Fun, Sometimes Silly, Romantic, To The Unique

The Dater's Handbook
Includes Dating Tips

Cyndi Haynes & Dale Edwards
Todd & Tweedworth Publishing

Published By

Todd & Tweedworth Publishing
5400 East Timberwood Drive
Newburgh, IN 47630

Printed in the United States of America

ISBN 0-9629118-0-1

Library of Congress Catalog Card Number

91-065299

DEDICATION

To Carol, Charles, Marme and Bubba who gave
me their unfailing support and love.

C.H.

ACKNOWLEDGMENTS

To Phil: Thanks for your invaluable
help and patience.

To Schelto: Thanks for all of your expert advice.

PREFACE

   Dating in the 90's is competitive, complex and constantly changing. This book, through its list of things to do on a date and its dating tips, will give you a superlative edge. Romance is back in style and more singles than ever are involved in the dating game. It is our goal to provide you with ideas that will rescue you from the "standard date" rut and make dating the wonderful and romantic adventure that it was meant to be.

   2002 Things To Do On A Date can be used in many ways. You can simply enjoy reading it and dream of the perfect date. You may choose to check the boxes of those things that you wish to do. You can use it to catalog the dates that you have tried by marking off those boxes. Or finally, you may choose to go through it with your special someone to plan your future dates.

   However you decide to use it, remember that this is a dating handbook that you can refer to again and again. Whether you are sixteen or seventy, just entering the dating scene or are an experienced dater, this book will give you more confidence, more polish and more fun in your love life!

                                                 Happy dating,

                                                 Cyndi & Dale

THE INGREDIENTS FOR A
PERFECT ROMANCE

1. Ride through the park after dark in a horse drawn carriage . . ☐

2. Kiss good night . . . . ☐

3. Discover an out of the way cafe . . . . ☐

4. Pray together . . . . ☐

5. Enjoy a sunset walk along the beach . . . . ☐

6. Pass love notes in the library . . . . ☐

7. Lend support during a tough time . . . . ☐

8. Hang mistletoe together . . . . ☐

9. Have "your table" at your favorite restaurant . . . . ☐

10. Sneak away for a moonlit swim . . . . ☐

11. Go to a local grove to pick fruit and then go
    home and cook something wonderful with it . . . . ☐

12. Flirt only with each other . . . . ☐

13. Snuggle up while listening to Linda Ronstadt
    with Nelson Riddle & His Orchestra . . . . ☐

14. Stop to make a purchase from a street flower vendor . . . . ☐

15. Share a bag of Hershey Kisses . . . . ☐

16. Snuggle . . . . ☐

17. Walk arm in arm on a foggy night . . . . ☐

18. Record a tape of your favorite songs . . . . ☐

19. Relax with a brandy by the fire . . . . ☐

1

20. Don't be too shy to act lovey-dovey . . . . ☐

21. Share a box of Godiva chocolates . . . . ☐

22. Go parking . . . . ☐

23. Steal a kiss while in a corner booth at a restaurant . . . . . . ☐

LET'S BE SPECTATORS!

24. Reserve side by side seats on the
    couch for Super Bowl Sunday . . . . ☐

25. For a panoramic view, climb a look-out tower . . . . ☐

26. Attend a golf tournament at a local club . . . . ☐

27. Catch the World Series . . . . ☐

28. Suffer through a slide presentation
    of your date's recent trip . . . . ☐

29. Check out jai alai . . . . ☐

30. Watch the pleasure boats scurrying about
    on the river on a hot Saturday afternoon . . . . ☐

31. Fall head over heels about each other at a diving meet . . . . ☐

32. Celebrate the arrival of spring with the Masters . . . . ☐

33. Gather at a sports bar to watch Monday night football . . . . ☐

34. Start the "wave" at a ball game . . . . ☐

35. Get reved up and watch the Indianapolis 500 . . . . ☐

36. Play lacrosse . . . . ☐

37. Host a Final Four party and serve a
    large pot of chili to get the ball rolling . . . . ☐

38. Watch the Tony Awards . . . . ☐

39. Have a fantastic time watching NBA basketball . . . . ☐

40. For two minutes of excitement, watch the Kentucky Derby . . ☐

REASONS WHY PEOPLE DATE

Companionship

To meet exciting people

All of your friends are dating

The world seems to be made for couples

To avoid loneliness

Friendship

Co-dependency

To find a spouse

All of your friends are married

It is a lot of fun

THE WORLD IS A BEAUTIFUL PLACE

41. Team up to wax your car in the park . . . . ☐

42. Have friends over for a backyard cook out . . . . ☐

43. Shape up and jog together . . . . ☐

44. Sit outside on the deck to enjoy
    a meal at a marina restaurant . . . . ☐

45. Make smores over the campfire . . . . ☐

46. Put the rest of the world on hold and
    take a leisurely walk through the woods . . . . ☐

47. Go deep sea diving to explore the underwater world . . . . . ☐

48. Shake the winter doldrums by shopping at a greenhouse . . . ☐

49. Visit a national park together . . . . ☐

50. Start the day off right with a sunrise picnic . . . . ☐

51. Stroll through a flower market together . . . . ☐

52. Try cross country skiing . . . . ☐

53. On an autumn day, treat yourselves
    to a covered bridge tour . . . . ☐

54. Enjoy the charm of a small fishing village . . . . ☐

55. Spend a sunny spring afternoon working in the garden . . . . ☐

56. Get away for a jeep ride in the desert . . . . ☐

57. Brighten your view of the world by planting a window box . . ☐

58. Wander through a botanical garden . . . . ☐

59. Make discoveries at a planetarium . . . . ☐

60. Try snorkeling . . . . ☐

61. Take a watercolor class together . . . . ☐

62. Spend the entire day whale watching . . . . ☐

63. Enjoy the view of your city from an overlook . . . . ☐

64. Enroll together in an art appreciation class . . . . ☐

65. Stroll through a campground . . . . ☐

66. Worship together at a sunrise service . . . . ☐

67. Make a stained glass window . . . . ☐

68. Explore a nature center . . . . ☐

69. For an investment in future scenery, plant bulbs . . . . . . ☐

70. Saunter along a brook . . . . ☐

71. Develop your creativity in a photography class . . . . ☐

72. Take a cog railroad ride . . . . ☐

73. Discover an all new world at a wildlife preservation . . . . . ☐

74. Enjoy the splendor of fall with a foliage drive . . . . ☐

PUTTIN' ON THE RITZ

75. Go all out and dine at a five star restaurant . . . . ☐

76. Get lost in the delightful sounds of a symphony concert . . . ☐

77. Join your friends for an event at a private club . . . . ☐

78. Celebrate a special occasion with a bottle of vintage wine . . ☐

79. Enjoy a relaxing evening with the philharmonic . . . . ☐

80. Enrich yourselves at a cathedral service . . . . ☐

81. Dress your best and go to a formal . . . . ☐

82. Drool through Saks Fifth Avenue . . . . ☐

83. Hire a violinist to play during dinner . . . . ☐

84. Rendezvous for a cup of tea at a grand hotel . . . . ☐

85. Have dinner in an elegant dining car . . . . ☐

86. Experience the magic of the opera . . . . ☐

87. Join in the celebration of a debutante ball . . . . ☐

88. Appreciate the grace and beauty of the ballet . . . . ☐

89. Feel the excitement of an opening night . . . . ☐

90. Ask your date out with a formal invitation . . . . ☐

91. Treat yourselves to a royal afternoon at a polo match . . . . ☐

92. Hobnob at a black tie dinner . . . . ☐

WEE HOUR HAPPENINGS

93. With a telescope, some munchies and a
warm blanket, watch for Halley's comet . . . . ☐

94. Attend a midnight mass together . . . . ☐

95. Go grocery shopping at 3:00 a.m. . . . . ☐

96. Cram for an exam . . . . ☐

97. Meet her after the guy's night out . . . . ☐

98. Go fishing together before the sun comes up . . . . ☐

99. After the party, stop for a post New Year's Eve breakfast . . . ☐

100. Share your thoughts and feelings about life after death . . . . ☐

101. Window shop after the stores have closed . . . . ☐

102. Visit an all night restaurant during the early morning hours . . ☐

103. Stay up and listen for Santa's reindeer . . . . ☐

104. Treat yourselves to a midnight snack . . . . ☐

105. Host a pajama party for your friends . . . . ☐

106. Hunt for bargains at a midnight madness sale . . . . ☐

107. Remember to turn back your clocks at 2:00 a.m. . . . . ☐

108. Night prowl . . . . □

109. Wait in line all night together for tickets . . . . □

110. Get a compass, drive a convertible, and hunt for UFOs . . . □

111. Enjoy a romantic moonlit picnic . . . . □

112. Kick off your shoes and wade knee-deep in a lake . . . . . □

113. For a long date, play the game of Monopoly . . . . □

> *To be loved, be lovable.*
> Ovid

HEART TO HEART

114. Make a New Year's resolution list together . . . . □

115. Share a root beer float . . . . □

116. Celebrate your good times (don't take them for granted) . . □

117. Hug . . . . □

118. Request "your song" on the radio . . . . □

119. Slow dance at a local club . . . . □

120. Serenade each other . . . . □

121. Help solve your problems by writing
a letter to Dear Abby together . . . . □

122. Whisper sweet nothings . . . . □

123. Read poetry to each other . . . . □

124. Share a brief version of your life story . . . . □

125. Take a snuggle break during a stressful time . . . . □

126. Celebrate Significant Other Day at the end of each month . . ☐

127. Pitch in to help each other solve a problem . . . . ☐

128. Share your true feelings . . . . ☐

PARTY TIME

129. Celebrate TGIF together . . . . ☐

130. Make new friends at a neighborhood party . . . . ☐

131. Host a Christmas in July party . . . . ☐

132. Attend a church social . . . . ☐

133. Address party invitations together
for your upcoming bash . . . . ☐

134. Accompany your date to their office party . . . .☐

135. Become entangled with the game of Twister . . . .☐

136. Throw a bon voyage party for your departing friends . . . . .☐

137. Loosen up and take disco lessons . . . .☐

138. Mix up your routine by taking a bartending class together . . ☐

139. Kick off an event with a pregame party . . . . ☐

140. Blow out your birthday candles and make a wish . . . . . .☐

141. Entertain country style with a barn dance . . . . ☐

142. Crash a formal party . . . .☐

143. Shake the winter doldrums by
hosting an indoor beach party . . . . ☐

144. Go to a Lion's Club dance . . . . ☐

145. Make future plans for the two
of you by replying to an RSVP . . . . ☐

146. Host a festive birthday party . . . . ☐

147. Go together to a family Memorial Day picnic . . . . ☐

148. Make candy apples to give away for Halloween treats . . . . ☐

ENJOY

149. Capture the taste of a fall festival . . . . ☐

150. Join in the festive spirit at your company Christmas party . . ☐

151. Read the Sunday comics together . . . . ☐

152. Meander back roads without any
particular destination in mind . . . . ☐

153. Relax yourselves in a hot tub . . . . ☐

154. Share an ice cream sandwich on a hot summer day . . . . . ☐

155. Get away for a day trip . . . . ☐

156. Take advantage of a windy March day
by sailing model boats on a lake . . . . ☐

157. Play footsies under the dinner table . . . . ☐

158. Celebrate the arrival of spring at an Easter parade . . . . . ☐

159. Trot on over to a horse show . . . . ☐

160. Read quietly side by side on the sofa . . . . ☐

161. Daydream the day away together . . . . ☐

162. Sightsee in a nearby town . . . . ☐

163. For a backyard feast, grill out steaks . . . . ☐

164. Take a ferryboat ride . . . . ☐

165. Listen and laugh to a comedy CD . . . . ☐

166. Leave your car at home and walk . . . . ☐

FIRST DATE ETIQUETTE

Dress accordingly

Consider your date's finances

Be up and positive

Don't drink too much

Keep your sense of humor

Remember that your date has feelings

Have the date well planned

Don't go to a singles' hangout

Tell your date what type of clothing to wear

Wear clothes that make you feel comfortable

Don't go anywhere that it is too loud to talk easily

Consider your date's interests

Thank the person at the end of the date

FROM LEFT FIELD

167. Fruitcake...bake it, eat it, throw the
     remainder away (this says it all) . . . . ☐

168. Cover the floor with newspapers
     and fingerpaint a masterpiece . . . . ☐

169. Watch a body building contest . . . . ☐

170. Try jujitsu . . . . ☐

171. For a change, listen to a foreign rock group . . . . ☐

172. Jump rope together for fitness . . . . ☐

173. Engage in a friendly pillow fight . . . . ☐

174. Act silly . . . . ☐

175. Celebrate Friday the 13th . . . . ☐

176. Have a fire escape picnic . . . . ☐

177. Make a meal entirely out of grocery store samples . . . . . ☐

178. Tune in MTV and join in with a kazoo . . . . ☐

179. Be adventurous and go to a accupuncture clinic . . . . . . ☐

180. Visit a stockyard . . . . ☐

181. Have a blast on Alamo Day . . . . ☐

182. Flip a coin to decide what to do on your date . . . . ☐

183. Tell your best UFO story . . . . ☐

184. Go out for a manicure for two . . . . ☐

185. Compare mood rings . . . . ☐

186. Don't just hang around the house
     all day, go bengee jumping . . . . ☐

187. Take harmonica lessons together . . . . ☐

188. Explore a spy store . . . . ☐

189. Beware of werewolves during a full moon . . . . ☐

190. Celebrate Dingus Day . . . . ☐

191. For a hoot, enter a hog calling contest . . . . ☐

192. Get your kicks by learning Tae Kwon Do . . . . ☐

193. Dine at a truck stop . . . . ☐

194. Form a Dead Poets' Society . . . . ☐

195. Be chauffeured on the waterways on a gondola . . . . . . ☐

196. View a foreign film . . . . ☐

197. Play an April Fool's Day prank . . . . ☐

198. Crash a large family reunion, then eat and run . . . . ☐

199. Hunt for bargains in a pawn shop . . . . ☐

200. Watch professional wrestling on television . . . . ☐

201. Host a gold fish race party . . . . ☐

202. Enjoy *The Far Side* . . . . ☐

203. Go Hawaiian by hosting a luau . . . . ☐

204. Watch a dog sled race . . . . ☐

205. Play with your pet rocks . . . . ☐

206. When the pace is too slow, pick
     it up by playing jacks again . . . . ☐

207. Enter a lip sinc contest . . . . ☐

208. Watch a belly dancer . . . . ☐

209. Tie die your t-shirts . . . . ☐

210. Engage yourselves in a competitive marbles match . . . . ☐

211. Be brave and try ski jumping . . . . ☐

212. For a cheap date, make a meal out
     of happy hour hor d'oeuvres . . . . ☐

213. Play Koosh ball . . . . ☐

214. Solve Rubik's Cube . . . . ☐

215. Stay on track by watching roller derby together . . . . ☐

216. Enjoy the ancient art of Bon Sai trees . . . . ☐

217. For self-defense and exercise, learn Kung Fu . . . . ☐

218. Head on to a demolition derby . . . . ☐

FOUR LEGGED FRIENDS LIKE DATING

219. Pick out your favorite pooch at a dog show . . . . ☐

220. Explore the countryside on horseback . . . . ☐

221. Grab your camera and go to the zoo for a great afternoon . . ☐

222. Bring home a doggy bag for your pet . . . . ☐

223. Jump at the opportunity to see an equestrian event . . . . . ☐

224. Visit a kennel and let a puppy steal your heart . . . . ☐

225. Look in the classified ads for a free
     kitten and bring home a new pal . . . . ☐

226. Take your dog for a walk in the park . . . . ☐

227. Introduce your date to your pets . . . . ☐

228. Feed the burnt piece of meat to the
     dog while the cook isn't looking . . . . ☐

229. Pick out winners together at the horse races . . . . ☐

230. Take a donkey ride along a mountain trail . . . . ☐

> *Spend more imagination than money.*
> Lyndon B. Johnson

AFTER 5:00 P.M.

231. Host a masquerade dinner for two . . . . ☐

232. For late night fun, go moonlight bowling . . . . ☐

233. Burn a yule log during the holidays . . . . ☐

234. For a quiet evening, go out for a glass
of wine and good conversation . . . . ☐

235. Watch an entire mini-series . . . . ☐

236. Splurge on an expensive, unforgettable night out . . . . . ☐

237. When the occasion calls for black tie attire, help him
shop for the perfect tuxedo and a fun cummerbund . . . . . ☐

238. Paint the town red together . . . . ☐

239. Host a dinner buffet for your favorite people . . . . ☐

240. Take your chances and throw a casino party . . . . ☐

241. Enjoy the lively atmosphere while dining at a supper club . . ☐

242. Relax and get caught up with each
other over drinks in a lounge . . . . ☐

243. Host a cocktail party together . . . . ☐

244. To make your date feel special,
order dinner for the two of you . . . . ☐

245. After the match, enjoy a meal at the tennis club . . . . . . ☐

246. Fraternize at a Moose Lodge function . . . . ☐

247. Celebrate by hosting a birthday dinner . . . . ☐

248. Mingle together at a bierstube . . . . ☐

249. Meet for a drink after work in an
elegant business district bar . . . . ☐

250. Exercise your rights and have an election night party . . . . ☐

251. Enjoy the view from a revolving bar . . . . ☐

252. Make the scene together at a fraternity or sorority dance . . ☐

HOME IS WHERE THE HEART IS

253. Shop at a second hand store to furnish his bachelor pad . . ☐

254. Spread a blanket on the living room
floor and have an indoor picnic . . . . ☐

255. Stay at home for the date . . . . ☐

256. For backyard fun, build a deck together . . . . ☐

257. Spend a Sunday afternoon touring the parade of homes . . ☐

258. Pop popcorn in the fireplace . . . . ☐

259. Steady your hands and build a house of cards . . . . ☐

260. Raid the refrigerator . . . . ☐

261. Build an unusual birdhouse to make
friends with some feathered creatures . . . . ☐

262. Host a "we finally completed the ..." party . . . . ☐

263. Lighten the load and help clean the house . . . . ☐

264. Close the curtains and play with your old set of tinkertoys . . ☐

265. Enjoy the charm of a historical house tour . . . . ☐

266. Throw a welcome home party for a pal . . . . ☐

267. Go ape and build a tree house . . . . ☐

268. If you like leftovers, have a casserole night at home . . . . . ☐

269. Go house hunting . . . . ☐

270. Try your hand at stenciling . . . . ☐

271. Invite your friends to a house painting party . . . . ☐

AN ENLIGHTENED DATE

272. Support your candidate of choice
by attending a political rally . . . . ☐

273. Quit smoking . . . . ☐

274. Keep up with currents events by watching
the local and national news together . . . . ☐

275. Role play to problem solve . . . . ☐

276. Watch your government at work
during a city council meeting . . . . ☐

277. Teach a Sunday school class together . . . . ☐

278. Philosophize the day away . . . . ☐

279. Enrich yourselves at a Maunday Thursday service . . . . . ☐

280. Examine the treasures at your local museum . . . . ☐

281. Take the MENSA test . . . . ☐

282. Start your pup off on the right paw and
take him to an obedience class together . . . . ☐

283. Have your cholesterol levels checked . . . . ☐

284. Watch PBS and learn while being entertained . . . . ☐

285. Attend your congressman's town meeting . . . . ☐

286. Improve yourselves with an image consultant . . . . ☐

287. Learn the facts about AIDS prevention . . . . ☐

288. Critique the play you have just seen over a late dinner . . . ☐

289. Look to the future by joining an investment club . . . . . . ☐

290. Spend an entire evening counting your blessings . . . . . ☐

291. Learn to be dynamic speakers
     at a Toastmaster's meeting . . . . ☐

292. Go to a biofeedback seminar . . . . ☐

293. Attend a news conference . . . . ☐

294. Critique the newest bestsellers . . . . ☐

295. Visit your city's visitor's bureau to
     discover something different to do . . . . ☐

296. Stay informed by attending a political speech . . . . ☐

PLACES TO MEET WOMEN

Co-ed hair salon	Education center
Craft fair	Cafe
Library	Church
On vacation	Workshop

FRED & GINGER WOULD BE PROUD

297. Teach each other to dance . . . . ☐

298. When you're too tired to be up on
     your feet, try finger dancing . . . . ☐

299. Start with the basics and learn the two step . . . . ☐

300. For fun and romance, go to a dance theater . . . . ☐

301. Attend a country club dance . . . . ☐

302. Get the fever on a Saturday night and go to a disco . . . . . ☐

303. Catch up with old friends at a homecoming dance . . . . . . ☐

304. Fast dance at a local hot spot . . . . ☐

305. Kick up your heels and join a dance club together . . . . . . ☐

306. Display your talents by entering a dance contest . . . . ☐

307. Make new friends at a cotillion . . . . ☐

308. Attend a dance recital . . . . ☐

309. Fox trot the night away . . . . ☐

310. Dress up and ballroom dance at home by candlelight . . . . ☐

311. Invent a new dance . . . . ☐

312. Watch a tap dancer perform . . . . ☐

MAKE THIS WORLD A LITTLE
BIT BETTER

313. Team up for volunteer church work . . . . ☐

314. Donate blood . . . . ☐

315. Rescue a puppy from the pound . . . . ☐

316. For added pocket change, recycle aluminum cans . . . . . . ☐

317. Support Big Brothers & Sisters . . . . ☐

318. Work on a project to save an animal
on the endangered species list . . . . ☐

319. Join a crusade to help the homeless . . . . ☐

320. Buy raffle tickets to support a good cause . . . . ☐

321. Improve your neighborhood by picking up litter . . . . . . ☐

322. Learn about saving our planet . . . . ☐

323. Do charity work and feel good about helping others . . . . ☐

324. Volunteer to assist the Special Olympics . . . . ☐

325. Give a little of your time to help the elderly . . . . ☐

326. Support a Humane Society event . . . . ☐

327. Volunteer to help at a soup kitchen . . . . ☐

328. Team up and write to a serviceman . . . . ☐

329. Stop by to brighten the day
of someone in a nursing home . . . . ☐

330. Adopt your own clean-up spot . . . . ☐

331. Shovel snow for a senior citizen . . . . ☐

332. Recycle newspapers . . . . ☐

333. Teach a child to read . . . . ☐

334. Celebrate Earth Day by improving our environment . . . . ☐

335. Join a worthwhile boycott . . . . ☐

336. Send a cow to Ethiopia (Heifer Project) . . . . ☐

337. Branch out from your routine by planting a tree . . . . . . ☐

MEETING SOMEONE NEW

Don't surround yourself by so many friends that you aren't
easy to approach

Smile, be friendly and initiate eye contact

Host a get-together and invite that person

I ONLY HAVE EYES FOR YOU

338. Celebrate Sweetest Day in October . . . . ☐

339. Bring in the new year with a romantic
New Year's Eve party for two . . . . ☐

340. Help your date select new eyeglass frames . . . . ☐

341. Talk about your previous relationships . . . . ☐

342. Model your new clothes to get your date's opinion . . . . . ☐

343. Read love poems to each other . . . . ☐

344. Steal a kiss while under the mistletoe . . . . ☐

345. Act silly and play hide and seek . . . . ☐

346. Read old cards and letters from each other to each other . . ☐

347. Cuddle . . . . ☐

348. Attend a beauty pageant together . . . . ☐

349. Ask him to a Sadie Hawkins dance . . . . ☐

350. Go flamingo dancing . . . . ☐

351. Drift off as you gaze into each other's eyes . . . . ☐

352. Buy matching funky sunglasses . . . . ☐

MUSIC SETS THE TONE

353. Get lost in the sounds of a violin concerto . . . . ☐

354. Take guitar lessons together . . . . ☐

355. Sing *Auld Lang Syne* at midnight . . . . ☐

356. For Nashville style fun, watch the Grand Ole Opry . . . . . . ☐

357. Play name that tune . . . . ☐

358. Sing along at a gospel concert . . . . ☐

359. Keep up with all the advances when
shopping for stereo equipment . . . . ☐

360. For a very relaxing evening, listen to chamber music . . . . ☐

361. Hit the trail to a country & western bar . . . . ☐

362. Spend an evening listening to your favorite albums . . . . . ☐

363. Drink in the soothing atmosphere of a jazz club . . . . . . ☐

364. Play a duet . . . . ☐

365. Have fun hooking up a new stereo system . . . . ☐

366. Listen to a religious radio station . . . . ☐

367. Discuss your musical likes and dislikes . . . . ☐

368. Audition a DJ for your party . . . . ☐

369. Go singing in the rain for a little romance . . . . ☐

370. Escape to another world at *Madame Butterfly* (opera) . . . . ☐

371. Display your talents by joining a glee club . . . . ☐

372. Shake your winter doldrums by listening
to the sound of the ocean in seashells . . . . ☐

WEEKEND WINNERS

373. For absolutely no reason at all, throw a party . . . . ☐

374. Catch a frisbee tournament . . . . ☐

375. With the classified ads in hand, spend a
Saturday afternoon searching for garage sales . . . . ☐

376. Join friends for a day of boating . . . . ☐

377. Team up to play in a couples' golf tournament . . . . ☐

378. Strawberries & cream and Wimbledon . . . . ☐

379. Enjoy watching little league baseball . . . . ☐

380. Be a sport and support a fund raiser . . . . ☐

381. Explore a street fair together . . . . ☐

382. Try adventure dining - look in the yellow pages
to discover a new restaurant and then go . . . . ☐

383. Play bocci ball . . . . ☐

384. Help each other find that perfect gift . . . . ☐

385. Watch a Sunday afternoon rugby match in the park . . . . . ☐

386. Host an indoor beach party during the winter . . . . ☐

387. Put on your best poker face for a battle of five card draw . . ☐

388. Relax at a coffee house . . . . ☐

389. Sit side by side on a park bench
and watch the world go by . . . . ☐

390. Count the cars on a passing train
when you are feeling impatient . . . . ☐

391. Kiss during red lights . . . . ☐

392. Work on a dude ranch for a day . . . . ☐

393. Have a ball at a tailgate party . . . . ☐

394. Get your kicks by taking a class to learn Karate . . . . ☐

395. Experience spiritual growth at a religious retreat . . . . . . ☐

396. Start a beer can collection together . . . . ☐

397. Cheer your friends on at a powderpuff football game . . . . ☐

398. Play a game of tennis . . . . ☐

399. Splish splash at a water park . . . . ☐

400. Try aerobics together . . . . ☐

401. Reach new depths in your
relationship, discover scuba diving . . . . ☐

402. Join a sports car club together . . . . ☐

COMMON DATING MISTAKES

Trying too hard

Running out of cash

Not making plans

Unrealistic expectations

Being too rigid

Leaving your sense of humor at home

Trying to make an old flame jealous

Making a date last too long

IT'S BETTER TO GIVE THAN TO RECEIVE

403. Pick out a name for your dog . . . . ☐

404. Celebrate Mother's Day by taking
your moms out to lunch together . . . . ☐

405. Attend a celebrity auction . . . . ☐

23

406. Hunt for an anniversary gift for a special couple . . . . . . ☐

407. Round up your friends for a wild west party . . . . ☐

408. Pitch in together to buy a birthday gift for a mutual friend . . ☐

409. Spend a Saturday afternoon shopping for Christmas gifts . . ☐

410. Shop together for that meaningful christening gift . . . . . . ☐

411. Give your own lie detector test . . . . ☐

412. Team up to throw a surprise party for a friend . . . . ☐

413. Have fun shopping together for a special baby gift . . . . . ☐

414. Do a good deed by signing up to be organ donors . . . . . ☐

415. Put your heads together to come up
with ideas for a unique graduation gift . . . . ☐

416. Host an around the world party . . . . ☐

417. Help find that "just right" Father's Day gift . . . . ☐

418. For your friends tying the knot, browse
the mall for a wedding present . . . . ☐

419. Help each other clean out closets and choose
which items to give to the Salvation Army . . . . ☐

ALL DRESSED UP

420. Be Romeo & Juliet at a "great couples" costume party . . . . ☐

421. Meet for drinks in an elegant hotel bar . . . . ☐

422. Take modeling lessons together . . . . ☐

423. Watch a New York haute couture
fashion show on television . . . . ☐

424. Buy matching t-shirts . . . . □

425. Help her pick out an Easter bonnet . . . . □

426. For that special look, try shopping
at a vintage clothing store . . . . □

427. Dress as cowpokes and go to a saloon . . . . □

428. Attempt to walk in snowshoes . . . . □

429. Give yourselves a boost by attending
a midweek church service . . . . □

430. Offer each other fashion advise . . . . □

431. Have a bum night - jeans, t-shirts and
spend no more than five dollars . . . . □

432. Host an elegant derby party, complete with mint juleps . . . □

433. Check out the new trends at a fashion show . . . . □

434. Enjoy a romantic dinner dance aboard a paddle wheeler . . □

435. Hobnob at a country club brunch . . . . □

436. Buy something fun and outrageous at a flea
market and wear it during your next date together . . . . . . □

> *Women fall in love through their ears
> and men through their eyes.*
> Woodrow Wyatt

MAYBE YOU COULD...

437. Listen to golden oldies . . . . □

438. Play a game of hearts - the only romantic card game . . . . □

439. Try to improve your game by watching the U.S. Open . . . . □

440. Have drinks at a riverboat bar . . . . ☐

441. In your spare time, play a game of miniature bowling . . . . ☐

442. Go to the hair stylist together for new "dos" . . . . ☐

443. Shoot baskets . . . . ☐

444. Discover the bargain of a lifetime at a condo auction . . . . . ☐

445. For a honey of a date, try beekeeping . . . . ☐

446. Go somewhere entirely new . . . . ☐

447. After a trip, greet your date at the
airport with a welcome home sign . . . . ☐

448. Decorate your house for autumn by making a scarecrow . . ☐

449. Attend a piano recital . . . . ☐

450. Get into shape by working out to an exercise video . . . . . ☐

451. Unwind together in a whirlpool . . . . ☐

452. Trot yourselves over to a harness race . . . . ☐

453. Take a class to learn a foreign language together . . . . . . ☐

454. Participate in a television auction . . . . ☐

455. Try a different kind of kiss - share a
bag of Hershey Kisses with almonds . . . . ☐

456. Build a ship in a bottle . . . . ☐

457. For breakfast anytime, try a meal at a pancake house . . . . ☐

458. Join in the festivities of a ribbon cutting ceremony . . . . . ☐

459. Enter a radio call-in contest . . . . ☐

460. Be prepared by earning your life
saving certificates together . . . . ☐

461. Feel patriotic while watching the Olympic games . . . . . ☐

462. Give your date a tote ride on your bike . . . . ☐

463. Capture your favorite spot on
canvas with your own oil paintings . . . . ☐

464. Search for hidden treasures with an old map . . . . ☐

465. Be brave and take diving lessons . . . . ☐

466. Enjoy the fresh air of a springtime lawn party . . . . ☐

467. Tell each other the gory details of your job . . . . ☐

468. Celebrate May Day by giving a beautiful spring bouquet . . ☐

469. Send a letter to the president . . . . ☐

470. See who can create the best culinary
masterpiece at a salad bar restaurant . . . . ☐

471. Sightsee by car in your city . . . . ☐

472. Observe Ash Wednesday . . . . ☐

473. Escape your day to day hassles
by playing the game of Life . . . . ☐

474. Join a debate team together . . . . ☐

475. Dine on crepes while watching the French Open . . . . . . ☐

476. Campaign for your favorite candidate . . . . ☐

477. Revive yourselves at a revival . . . . ☐

478. Tour a college campus . . . . ☐

479. Watch a gymnastics meet . . . . ☐

480. Be clowns in a children's hospital . . . . ☐

481. Experience a fine meal at a German restaurant . . . . ☐

```
┌─────────────────────────────────────────────────┐
│                                                 │
│      TO BE SUCCESSFUL AT THE DATING GAME        │
│                                                 │
│         Promptly return all phone calls         │
│                                                 │
│               Don't play games                  │
│                                                 │
│                   Be fun                        │
│                                                 │
│               Keep your word                    │
│                                                 │
│        Learn to be a good host/hostess          │
│                                                 │
│              Use good grammar                   │
│                                                 │
│        Learn to bring out the best in others    │
│                                                 │
│            Be adept at meeting people           │
│                                                 │
│         Don't lose touch with your friends      │
│                                                 │
│       Be willing to get out in the dating world │
│                                                 │
│            Have friends of both sexes           │
│                                                 │
│            Go places where singles go           │
│                                                 │
│            Don't be a couch potato              │
│                                                 │
│               Use good manners                  │
│                                                 │
│          Be involved in your community          │
│                                                 │
└─────────────────────────────────────────────────┘
```

HAIL HAIL THE GANG'S ALL HERE

482. Gather with friends to watch the All Star game . . . . ☐

483. Host an anniversary party for your folks . . . . ☐

484. Pass the afternoon by playing touch football . . . . ☐

485. Suffer together through a family reunion . . . . ☐

486. Invite your friends over for cocktails . . . . ☐

487. Host a Saturday brunch . . . . ☐

488. Recruit your pals to help support your favorite charity . . . . ☐

489. Mingle through the crowd at a fraternity party . . . . ☐

490. Make nachos for the gang . . . . ☐

491. Pick up a keg of beer and have your
friends drop by for an impromptu party . . . . ☐

492. Take your pets along for a day at the beach . . . . ☐

493. Throw a BYOD (donation) bash
to support a worthy cause . . . . ☐

494. Team up as partners to play Euchre . . . . ☐

495. Host a cocktail buffet . . . . ☐

496. Eliminate having to decorate for your
party by renting the entire museum . . . . ☐

497. Put in face time together at a friend's party . . . . ☐

498. When your gang has outgrown your
living room, have a garage party . . . . ☐

IF YOU DON'T KNOW ALL
THAT THERE IS TO KNOW

499. Prepare for your financial future by
enrolling in an investment class together . . . . ☐

500. Hold a Bible study . . . . ☐

501. Play the dictionary game . . . . ☐

502. Learn to make beautiful music
together by taking piano lessons . . . . ☐

503. Relax at a stress management seminar . . . . ☐

504. Take a correspondence course together . . . . ☐

505. Improve your frame of mind by
listening to a motivational tape . . . . □

506. Learn to keep score in the program at a baseball game . . . □

507. Keep up with the times by taking a computer class . . . . . □

508. Discover more about yourselves with
the results from an aptitude test . . . . □

509. Take voice lessons together . . . . □

510. Learn to oil paint . . . . □

511. Read and be amazed with the *Guinness Book of Records* . . □

512. Be comfortable at a Dale Carnegie training class . . . . . . □

513. Learn to drive a standard shift car . . . . □

514. Enroll in a class together at the YMCA . . . . □

IN THE OLD DAYS THEY DID...

515. Spend a Saturday afternoon
making homemade ice cream . . . . □

516. Go to your county fair . . . . □

517. For a relaxing evening, listen to classical music . . . . . . □

518. Bake a pie together . . . . □

519. Learn to waltz . . . . □

520. Refresh yourselves with fresh squeezed lemonade . . . . . □

521. Snuggle on a hayride . . . . □

522. Harvest your garden and can the fresh vegetables . . . . . □

523. Make your own Christmas ornaments . . . . □

524. Join a square dance club . . . . ☐

525. Watch a silent film and enjoy talking
through a movie for a change . . . . ☐

526. Roast marshmallows over the fire . . . . ☐

527. Throw horseshoes . . . . ☐

528. Cruise down the river aboard a paddle wheeler . . . . . . ☐

529. Try your hand at wood carving . . . . ☐

530. Make homemade jam together
to give away as a special gift . . . . ☐

531. Explore a spooky ghost town . . . . ☐

532. Listen to folk music to learn of local lore . . . . ☐

533. After a summertime rainstorm, make mud pies . . . . . . ☐

534. Watch a bicycle race . . . . ☐

535. Tell knock-knock jokes . . . . ☐

536. Have a box lunch date . . . . ☐

537. Roller skate . . . . ☐

538. Share the shade under an oak tree on a hot summer day . . ☐

539. Stroll a fairground . . . . ☐

540. Hunt for goodies at a bake sale . . . . ☐

541. Host a Memorial Day picnic for your neighborhood . . . . . ☐

542. Compete at card games . . . . ☐

543. Snuggle during a sleigh ride to grandmother's house . . . . ☐

544. Enter your best leaper in a frog race . . . . ☐

545. Fight high prices by planting your own vegetable garden . . ☐

546. After the movie, stop for a milkshake . . . . ☐

547. Have fun at a sweet sixteen birthday party . . . . ☐

548. String popcorn for the Christmas tree . . . . ☐

549. Throw an old fashioned hoedown . . . . ☐

550. Take turns on a tire swing . . . . ☐

551. Go strawberry picking . . . . ☐

552. Enjoy the beauty of church bells at Christmastime . . . . . . ☐

COURTING IN STYLE

553. Prepare an elaborate gourmet meal together . . . . ☐

554. Hire an accordion player to entertain during dinner . . . . . ☐

555. Read the collected works of Elizabeth Barrett Browning . . . ☐

556. Impress your date by ordering
     the meal in a foreign language . . . . ☐

557. Float away on a hot air balloon . . . . ☐

558. Dress up for an evening at home . . . . ☐

559. Sip hot cider with cinnamon by the fire . . . . ☐

560. Drink in the fresh air while dining on the patio . . . . ☐

561. Have a friend chauffeur you and your
     date around for the evening . . . . ☐

562. Reserve a private dining room for a dinner for two . . . . . ☐

563. Celebrate with Dom Perignon . . . . ☐

564. Spend the entire evening savoring a
     seven course meal at an elegant restaurant . . . . ☐

565. Enjoy the magic of a candlelight picnic . . . . ☐

566. Toast each other with soft drinks in champagne flutes . . . . ☐

567. Read Emily Post together to improve your manners . . . . . ☐

568. Delight in the ambience of a French restaurant . . . . ☐

**PEOPLE THAT MIGHT INTRODUCE YOU
TO AVAILABLE SINGLES**

Co-workers

Neighbors

Minister

Friends

Siblings

Aunts/Uncles

High school friends

College chums

Doctor

Sorority/Fraternity pals

SPORTSMAN'S CHOICE

569. Go deep sea fishing for a whale of a time . . . . ☐

570. For an adventurous day of exercising, go mountain biking . . ☐

571. Experience the exhilaration of white water rafting . . . . . . ☐

572. Visit a stable (better watch where you step) . . . . ☐

573. Be a pair of early birds when shopping
for supplies at a bait and tackle store . . . . ☐

574. Fish for compliments . . . . ☐

575. If you are tired of the ups and downs
of everyday life, try rappelling . . . .☐

576. Take riding lessons together . . . .☐

577. Dive for a sunken treasure . . . .☐

578. Introduce your date to snipe hunting . . . .☐

579. Relax on an inner tube float trip . . . .☐

580. For a guaranteed lift, join a ski club together . . . .☐

581. Get out and enjoy the fresh air while mountain climbing . . .☐

582. Be prepared and buy your fishing licenses . . . .☐

583. Browse a sporting goods store . . . .☐

SCHOOL BELLS

584. Attend your high school reunion together . . . .☐

585. Lend a hand to help address graduation announcements . .☐

586. Watch your favorite college sports team in action . . . . .☐

587. Work on a term paper together . . . .☐

588. To help ease the tension, go to a finals week party . . . . .☐

589. Visit your old school playground . . . .☐

590. Get fired up and go to a pep rally . . . .☐

591. Check out several colleges while trying
to decide which one is right for you . . . .☐

592. Celebrate Class Day together . . . .☐

593. Team up to work on a school project . . . .☐

594. Shop for supplies at a back to school sale . . . . ☐

595. Browse the bookstore together . . . . ☐

596. Eliminate the decision of what
to wear by throwing a toga party . . . . ☐

597. Participate together in coed intramural sports . . . . ☐

598. Join in the celebration of a graduation party . . . . ☐

599. Get involved by attending a PTA function . . . . ☐

600. Talk about your day at school . . . . ☐

601. Discover an out of the way spot for a campus picnic . . . . . ☐

602. Wear your old letter sweater and
go to a high school sporting event . . . . ☐

603. See a college play together . . . . ☐

604. Check out a Union Board happening . . . . ☐

605. Attend a high school graduation ceremony . . . . ☐

GETTING TO KNOW YOU

606. Do nothing but chat and get
acquainted without distractions . . . . ☐

607. Share your personal beliefs . . . . ☐

608. Offer a shoulder to lean on during a difficult time . . . . . . ☐

609. Give the grand tour of your work place . . . . ☐

610. Talk about your childhood heroes and heroines . . . . ☐

611. Play the "what if" game and be careful
how you answer the questions . . . . ☐

612. Clean up your act by doing your laundry together ...... ☐

613. Watch home movies .... ☐

614. Show off your collections and treasured mementos ..... ☐

615. Compare fortune cookies .... ☐

616. Look through family photo albums .... ☐

617. Learn about each other's character
     by playing the game of Scruples .... ☐

618. Talk about your favorite hobbies .... ☐

619. Reveal your "most embarrassing" story .... ☐

620. Play the game of 20 questions .... ☐

621. Share some of your secrets .... ☐

622. Read *The Book of Questions* by Gregory Stock, Ph.D. ... ☐

**HOW TO TELL IF YOUR RELATIONSHIP IS ON THE
DOWNHILL CURVE**

You don't look forward to seeing each other anymore

You are bored on dates

You feel stifled

Your friends tell you to move on with your life

You no longer look for reasons to call

You feel that you need more time apart

A date seems to last forever

You'd rather be home alone than with your date

Little things about the other person are
starting to bug you in a big way

OUT ON THE TOWN

623. Treat yourselves to an evening at the theater . . . . ☐

624. Spice up your life by trying Cajun cooking . . . . ☐

625. Meet for an early morning walk . . . . ☐

626. Enjoy an ethnic festival . . . . ☐

627. Join your grandparents for a
Friday night at the VFW Post . . . . ☐

628. Attend a Pops concert . . . . ☐

629. Kick off your shoes and enjoy
yourselves at a Japanese restaurant . . . . ☐

630. Join a protest march . . . . ☐

631. Meet your parents for cocktails . . . . ☐

632. Brush up on your knowledge of history
by visiting a historical monument . . . . ☐

633. Stop by a marina to enjoy the view . . . . ☐

634. While walking downtown, treat
yourselves to a street vendor meal . . . . ☐

635. Experience the excitement of Chinatown . . . . ☐

636. Dress as a tourist and take pictures
of the two of you all over town . . . . ☐

637. Collect cocktail napkins of places
that you have been together . . . . ☐

638. For country dwellers, spend a day in the city . . . . ☐

639. Celebrate with the winners and cry
with the losers at an election night party . . . . ☐

640. Meet new people at a black tie cocktail party . . . . ☐

641. Try an ethnic food that neither
one of you have had before . . . . ☐

642. Pick up a carry out dinner and
enjoy it at your favorite spot . . . . ☐

OUR PARENTS USED TO...

643. Take a Sunday afternoon drive . . . . ☐

644. Play checkers . . . . ☐

645. Swallow goldfish . . . . ☐

646. Stroll through a formal garden . . . . ☐

647. Spend the day at a carnival . . . . ☐

648. Walk her home after school and carry her books . . . . . . ☐

649. To satisfy your sweet tooth, make candy . . . . ☐

650. Play croquet on the front lawn . . . . ☐

651. Host a hillbilly party . . . . ☐

652. Relax at a Labor Day picnic . . . . ☐

653. Jitterbug the night away . . . . ☐

654. Dress up in fabulous costumes for a Halloween party . . . . ☐

655. Play shuffleboard . . . . ☐

656. After church, enjoy a fried chicken dinner . . . . ☐

657. Stroll through the midway at a fair . . . . ☐

658. Order a cherry coke with two straws . . . . ☐

659. For a date that is right on target, throw darts . . . . ☐

660. Make a paper garland for the Christmas tree . . . . ☐

661. Play Parchesi . . . . ☐

662. Listen to your echoes in a cave . . . . ☐

663. Do the twist . . . . ☐

664. Ride around town in a street car . . . . ☐

665. Enjoy a Sunday afternoon double feature . . . . ☐

666. Play bridge . . . . ☐

667. Strike out of your regular routine and go bowling . . . . . ☐

668. Keep your fingers crossed for a white Christmas . . . . . ☐

669. Have a coffee date . . . . ☐

TIME MARCHES ON

670. Run in a marathon race together . . . . ☐

671. Tour a historic log cabin . . . . ☐

672. Start the year off right by
attending a New Year's Day party . . . . ☐

673. Return overdue library books . . . . ☐

674. You and your date can pow-wow at an Indian reservation . . ☐

675. Beachcomb together . . . . ☐

676. Attend a civil war reenactment . . . . ☐

677. Stroll along the boardwalk hand in hand . . . . ☐

678. Go to a marching band show . . . . ☐

679. Be lazy together . . . . ☐

680. Get away from the rat race by visiting an Amish village . . . ☐

681. Team up to throw a graduation party . . . . ☐

682. Attend a wake . . . . ☐

683. Celebrate the shortest day of the year - December 21st . . . ☐

684. For an endurance date, enter a dance marathon contest . . ☐

685. Capture days gone by at a historical park . . . . ☐

686. Co-host a retirement party for a special friend . . . . ☐

687. Learn to dance the Charleston . . . . ☐

> Love does not consist in gazing at each other but
> in looking together in the same direction.
> Antoine de Saint-Exupery

THE BEST THINGS IN LIFE ARE FREE

688. Run barefoot through the park . . . . ☐

689. Stay until the last ember in the fireplace goes out . . . . . . ☐

690. Wander the heavens while looking
through a telescope at the stars . . . . ☐

691. Wade knee-deep in a fountain . . . . ☐

692. Dance at home to the radio . . . . ☐

693. Watch future superstars at a little league football game . . . ☐

694. Bathe your dog together . . . . ☐

695. Bundle up and build a snowman . . . . ☐

696. Turn off all the room lighting and capture
the quiet splendor of a lit Christmas tree . . . . ☐

697. Try snow painting . . . . ☐

698. Relax at a Sunday afternoon concert in the park . . . . . . ☐

699. Worship together at a small country church . . . . ☐

700. Go horseback riding on the beach . . . . ☐

701. Skate without skates after an ice storm . . . . ☐

702. People watch at the mall . . . . ☐

703. Cheer at a little league soccer game . . . . ☐

704. Catch some rays together . . . . ☐

705. With lawn chairs in hand, go early to
get a good spot to enjoy a local parade . . . . ☐

706. Sing together in church . . . . ☐

707. Spend a spring afternoon bird watching . . . . ☐

708. Make snow ice cream . . . . ☐

THE MORE THE MERRIER

709. Attend your company picnic and show off your date . . . . . ☐

710. Warm up with a chili dinner on a cold night . . . . ☐

711. Throw a BYOB/BYOG party (old boyfriends & girlfriends)
to introduce your single friends to each other . . . . ☐

712. Accompany your date to a reception . . . . ☐

713. Join the fun at your niece or nephew's first birthday party . . ☐

714. Enjoy a 50th wedding anniversary celebration . . . . ☐

715. Host a wine tasting party . . . . ☐

716. For a bow-wow bonanza, throw
a birthday party for your dog . . . . ☐

717. Dress warmly for a winter party on the beach . . . . ☐

718. Plan your guest list for a joint party . . . . ☐

719. Play charades . . . . ☐

720. Mingle together at an office party . . . . ☐

721. Celebrate the birthday of a friend . . . . ☐

722. Share in the excitement of an
engagement announcement party . . . . ☐

723. Put in an appearance at your parent's open house . . . . . ☐

724. With steady hands, stack dominoes . . . . ☐

725. Blimey, why not host a St. Patrick's Day party? . . . . . . ☐

THE MOST WONDERFUL
TIME OF THE YEAR

726. Spend a delightful evening decorating the Christmas tree . . ☐

727. Celebrate the last day of school together . . . . ☐

728. Get into the holiday spirit by listening to Christmas music . . ☐

729. Feel the excitement and joy of an Easter service . . . . . . ☐

730. Dream of fabulous gifts under your tree
as you window shop at Christmastime . . . . ☐

731. Prepare a holiday feast together . . . . ☐

732. Share your memories of past holidays . . . . ☐

733. Celebrate New Year's Eve at home together . . . . □

734. Get together with good friends
for a special Christmas party . . . . □

735. Go panic shopping together on December 24th . . . . . . □

736. Enjoy a picnic in the snow with candles,
hot chocolate and your date to keep you warm . . . . . . □

737. Kick up your heels at a spring dance . . . . □

738. Watch *A Christmas Carol* to
catch the spirit of the holidays . . . . □

739. Spend a fall afternoon raking leaves together . . . . □

740. Select a Christmas tree and try not to
get one that looks like Charlie Brown's . . . . □

741. Eat sauerkraut on New Year's Day for good luck . . . . . . □

742. Fight the crowds together the day after
Thanksgiving (the busiest day of the year) . . . . □

743. Make Easter baskets for underprivileged kids . . . . □

744. Share egg nog by the tree . . . . □

745. Go to a Christmas tree show to gather
ideas on how to decorate your tree . . . . □

746. Watch the parades together on Thanksgiving Day . . . . . □

747. Browse a Christmas store to find that special ornament . . . □

748. Spend a snow day together . . . . □

749. See *The Nutcracker Suite* at Christmastime . . . . □

750. Dress in festive evening clothing
to attend a holiday dance . . . . □

751. Take down your Christmas tree together to make
what would have been a sad occasion a fun one . . . . . . □

```
┌─────────────────────────────────────────────┐
│                                             │
│   COMPONENTS OF A QUALITY RELATIONSHIP      │
│              Worship together               │
│                 Honesty                     │
│                 Loyalty                     │
│               Compassion                    │
│                Friendship                   │
│                  Love                       │
│               Sensitivity                   │
│              A sense of fun                 │
│              Understanding                  │
│                Admiration                   │
│                 Respect                     │
│                  Trust                      │
│             Faith in each other             │
│               Commitment                    │
│                                             │
└─────────────────────────────────────────────┘
```

SURF'S UP

752. Set sail on a rented pontoon boat . . . . ☐

753. Grab a bite to eat while poolside . . . . ☐

754. Go to a seafood restaurant and
     select your own lobster for dinner . . . . ☐

755. On a hot day, push your date into the pool (and then run) . . ☐

756. Experience the exhilaration of speedboating . . . . ☐

757. Take off for a day cruise . . . . ☐

758. Enjoy a picnic at the beach . . . . ☐

759. Go swimming on New Year's Day
with the Polar Bear Club . . . . ☐

760. Search for pearls in oysters . . . . ☐

761. Browse a boat show . . . . ☐

762. Go to a swim meet . . . . ☐

763. Dine at a seaside restaurant . . . . ☐

764. Hang ten while surfing . . . . ☐

765. Sand, sun, friends, food and drink -
the ingredients for a super beach party . . . . ☐

766. Have a water balloon fight . . . . ☐

767. Keep cool while sunbathing in a baby pool . . . . ☐

768. Charter a boat for an aquatic adventure . . . . ☐

769. Spend the afternoon at a river camp . . . . ☐

770. Discover a picturesque spot at the lake and etch . . . . . ☐

771. Visit a lighthouse on a foggy night . . . . ☐

772. Go exploring in a glass bottom boat . . . . ☐

773. For your seafood lover friends, host a clambake . . . . . . ☐

774. Jump into the fun at your neighborhood pool . . . . ☐

775. Be entertained with the show at a water theme park . . . . ☐

776. Take swimming lesson together . . . . ☐

777. Have fun, fun, fun, listening to the Beach Boys . . . . ☐

IT TAKES TWO

778. Play racquetball for a good work out . . . . ☐

779. Split a banana split . . . . ☐

780. Team up to entertain together . . . . ☐

781. Enjoy an autumn day paddle boating . . . . ☐

782. Learn to play chess . . . . ☐

783. Even at the risk of getting egg on
your face, enter an egg toss contest . . . . ☐

784. Share a hymnal . . . . ☐

785. Role play to prepare for a job interview . . . . ☐

786. Try fencing . . . . ☐

787. Practice for a kissing marathon . . . . ☐

788. Play table shuffleboard . . . . ☐

789. Engage in a battle of laser tag . . . . ☐

790. Give her a piggy back ride . . . . ☐

791. Share an umbrella during a thunderstorm . . . . ☐

792. Play ping-pong . . . . ☐

793. Prevent sunburn - put suntan lotion on each other . . . . . ☐

794. Play pitch & catch in the backyard . . . . ☐

795. Snap photos of each other . . . . ☐

796. Play foosball . . . . ☐

797. Frame a picture together at a frame it yourself shop . . . . . ☐

798. Win at double solitaire (without cheating) . . . . ☐

799. Enjoy an afternoon of backgammon . . . . ☐

800. Don't waste food, share a Chinese meal . . . . ☐

801. Teeter-totter an evening away . . . . ☐

802. To prevent chapped lips, try Eskimo kissing . . . . ☐

803. Enjoy Chateaubriand for two . . . . ☐

804. Play air hockey . . . . ☐

DATING IN THE WORK PLACE

Check office policy

Use discretion

Be prepared for office gossip

Avoid PDA (Public Display of Affection)

Examine your own motives for dating this person

Consider whether your career would
suffer if the relationship ended

GETTING BACK TO NATURE

805. Explore an unknown path through the woods . . . . ☐

806. Take a portable grill to the park and fix a fun feast . . . . . . ☐

807. Dodge raindrops together . . . . ☐

808. Break through your winter routine by trying ice fishing . . . . ☐

809. Spend a day on a farm . . . . ☐

810. Celebrate the arrival of spring by hosting a garden party . . ☐

811. Play in a summer rain shower . . . . ☐

812. Take a stroll through the woods to pick wild flowers . . . . . ☐

813. Warm your fingers and toes at a winter wiener roast . . . . . ☐

814. Enjoy the quiet beauty of a sunrise . . . . ☐

815. See how many times that you can
make a rock skip across a pond . . . . ☐

816. Plant next year's Christmas tree . . . . ☐

817. Chase butterflies . . . . ☐

818. Rejuvenate yourselves at a mineral spring . . . . ☐

819. Try rock collecting (we recommend diamonds) . . . . ☐

820. Run barefoot on the beach . . . . ☐

821. If you live in the city, spend an entire day in the country . . . ☐

822. Explore a national forest . . . . ☐

823. Sneak away for an outdoor nap . . . . ☐

824. Gather pine cones for your Christmas decorations . . . . . ☐

825. Enjoy hiking for the exercise and fresh air . . . . ☐

826. Dig up night crawlers for fishing bait . . . . ☐

827. Spend an afternoon picking wild mushrooms . . . . ☐

828. Team up to chaperone a church youth camp out . . . . . . ☐

THERE'S MAGIC IN THE AIR

829. Ask your date out in a spectacular
way by hiring a skywriter . . . . ☐

830. Every 76 years, host a Halley's Comet party . . . . ☐

831. Leave the hustle and bustle
behind and float away in a glider . . . . ☐

832. Race pigeons . . . . ☐

833. Arrive in time for a farewell drink at an airport private club . . ☐

834. Soar off to an aviation show . . . . ☐

835. Chase rainbows together . . . . ☐

836. Pack a cooler and take lawn chairs
along to watch a volcano erupt . . . . ☐

837. Get up the nerve to try skydiving . . . . ☐

838. Take a helicopter ride and enjoy the view . . . . '. . ☐

839. Catch some rays on the roof of a skyscraper . . . . ☐

840. Let your minds soar while enjoying a balloon race . . . . . . ☐

841. Set the mood by burning incense . . . . ☐

842. Wish upon a shooting star . . . . '. . . . . ☐

843. Let your minds wander off as you star gaze together . . . . ☐

844. Act crazy by riding up and down in a glass
elevator several times while enjoying the view . . . . ☐

845. Go plane watching at the airport late at night . . . . ☐

846. Enter a kite flying contest . . . . ☐

847. Entertain your friends at a rooftop party . . . . ☐

848. Challenge each other to a
watermelon seed spitting contest . . . . ☐

849. Lie on your back and pick out cloud formations . . . . ☐

850. To avoid the risk of blindness, keep your
eyes closed and kiss during a solar eclipse . . . . ☐

851. Be amazed at a magic show . . . . ☐

COMMUNICATION IS THE KEY

852. Attend a writing workshop together . . . . ☐

853. Phone date . . . . ☐

854. Talk in a foreign language for the entire date . . . . ☐

855. Go to a prayer meeting . . . . ☐

856. Learn Braille together . . . . ☐

857. Give hints about what you want for Christmas . . . . ☐

858. Give hints about the Christmas gifts that you've bought . . . ☐

859. Complete a self help magazine questionnaire . . . . ☐

860. Be a good sport and listen to
your date practice their speech . . . . ☐

861. Take a sign language class together . . . . ☐

862. Team up to create doodle art . . . . ☐

863. Call your good buddies on a CB radio . . . . ☐

864. Write a letter to your congressman . . . . ☐

865. Dazzle your date with your knowledge of trivia . . . . ☐

866. Take a calligraphy class . . . . ☐

867. Teach a bird to talk . . . . ☐

COZY CORNER

868. Warm up with hot cocoa and a blanket on a cold night . . . ☐

869. Discover a quaint country cafe . . . . ☐

870. Share a lazy Sunday evening on the porch swing . . . . . ☐

871. Read a good mystery novel together and solve it . . . . . ☐

872. Build a gingerbread house . . . . ☐

873. Take a break from a hectic day to
enjoy a private picnic in your office . . . . ☐

874. Sip an after dinner liqueur . . . . ☐

875. Savor quiet time together after a long and busy day . . . . . ☐

876. Hang Christmas stockings with care . . . . ☐

877. Be couch potatoes together . . . . ☐

878. Spend a morning browsing through
magazines at a newsstand . . . . ☐

879. Curl up together next to a window and watch it snow . . . . ☐

880. Host a small intimate dinner party . . . . ☐

881. The perfect snack - hot cocoa and
animal crackers on a winter evening . . . . ☐

882. Share part of yourself during a fireside chat . . . . ☐

883. Orchestrate a coffee break from work together . . . . ☐

DATING SAFETY

Meet at a neutral place the first time or two

Always have your own transportation

Pick a place to meet with which you are familiar

Meet in a public spot that is well lighted

Let a friend know where you are and when you will be home

THE COUPLE THAT PLAYS TOGETHER
STAYS TOGETHER

884. Join a coed volleyball league . . . . ☐

885. Play Putt-Putt . . . . ☐

886. Have a snowball fight . . . . ☐

887. Perform your best card tricks and then
share the secret of how it is done . . . . ☐

888. Head for the slopes to snow ski . . . . ☐

889. Compete at gin rummy . . . . ☐

890. Learn to play paddleball . . . . ☐

891. Be co-owners in a fantasy sports league . . . . ☐

892. Challenge each other at Ninetendo . . . . ☐

893. Play on a coed softball team . . . . ☐

894. Chill out together on a hot summer
day by going swimming . . . . ☐

895. Build a snow fort . . . . ☐

896. Risk your fortunes at penny-ante poker . . . . ☐

897. Learn to play squash . . . . ☐

898. Try your hand at handball . . . . ☐

899. Frolic at the bottom of a waterfall . . . . ☐

900. Join a mixed bowling league . . . . ☐

901. Play tic-tac-toe to determine who will
pay for dinner (best two out of three) . . . . ☐

> *The best gifts are tied with heartstrings .*
> Anonymous

THE STUFF DREAMS ARE MADE OF

902. Make your Christmas lists . . . . ☐

903. Tour a local mansion and imagine what your
     lives would have been like had you lived there . . . . ☐

904. Attend a jewelry auction . . . . ☐

905. Throw coins in a wishing well . . . . ☐

906. Share the fantasy of how you would
     spend a million dollars in one week . . . . ☐

907. Show off your trophies and awards . . . . ☐

908. Delight in a Neiman Marcus Christmas catalog . . . . . . ☐

909. Enter a comedy search contest at a night club . . . . ☐

910. Share your life long dreams . . . . ☐

911. Dress up and shop for something that you can't afford . . . . ☐

912. Team up to devise a fabulous money making project . . . . ☐

913. Window shop elegant stores . . . . ☐

914. Check out the new sports cars at an auto show . . . . . . ☐

915. Nap on a lap . . . . ☐

916. Saunter through a chic boutique . . . . ☐

917. Make a birthday wish list . . . . ☐

918. Share your career goals . . . . ☐

919. Determine how to spend your future
     lottery winnings (just in case) . . . . ☐

920. Beat the rush and go early to pan for gold . . . . ☐

FOR THE YOUNG AT HEART

921. Take a walk in the magical
     world after a late night snowfall . . . . ☐

922. Host a special birthday party (16th, 21st, 30th...) . . . . . . ☐

923. Venture to the park together on a cold
     night with a thermos of hot chocolate . . . . ☐

924. Kidnap the other from work . . . . ☐

925. Try your hand at snow sculpting . . . . ☐

926. Go trick or treating again . . . . ☐

927. Throw coins in a fountain and hope
     that your dreams will come true . . . . ☐

928. Relax on a riverboat cruise . . . . ☐

929. Spend a carefree day lounging by the pool . . . . ☐

930. Be silly together in a photo booth
     and capture the fun on film . . . . ☐

931. Buy Cracker Jacks and hunt for the prize . . . . ☐

932. Be brave and try something
     totally outrageously adventurous . . . . ☐

933. Cooking 101...Slice & Bake cookies . . . . ☐

934. Make funny faces at the chimps in the zoo . . . . ☐

935. Go sledding on a Saturday morning . . . . ☐

936. Visit a comic book dealer and be amazed at how expensive your old comics are today ☐

937. Share a bag of gummy bears ☐

938. Act like kids again and watch a Disney classic ☐

939. Show off your yo-yo tricks ☐

940. Browse an antique toy fair ☐

941. Build a clubhouse for a little friend ☐

942. Spend an entire afternoon at the arcade ☐

943. Challenge each other to a sidewalk tic-tac-toe match ☐

944. Play crazy eights ☐

945. Look through your childhood books together and reminisce ☐

946. Build a model ☐

947. Visit a petting zoo ☐

948. Try to get a boomerang to work ☐

949. Ride the kiddie train around the zoo ☐

950. Blow bubbles and imagine you're on the *Lawrence Welk Show* ☐

951. Build an intricate dollhouse ☐

952. Stay up late to watch for Santa ☐

953. Browse a toy store and relive the wonderful magic of childhood ☐

954. Watch the Harlem Globetrotters ☐

955. Compete at video games ☐

956. Have fun at the circus again ☐

HOSTING A DINNER DATE

Make something that will allow you to spend time with your date and not the entire time in the kitchen

Set an attractive table

Clean your place beforehand

Allow time before the meal for a drink and conversation

Make your date feel comfortable in your home

Cook something that you have had success with in the past

If the results don't turn out as planned, have a "Plan B" ready

BIRDS OF A FEATHER FLOCK TOGETHER

957. Join a bicycle club together and enjoy touring the countryside . . . . ☐

958. Flock to a pet store to buy a bird . . . . ☐

959. Be adventurous and charter a plane . . . . ☐

960. Join the MUFONS . . . . ☐

961. Contribute to a worthy cause . . . . ☐

962. Play badminton . . . . ☐

963. Get wild and become involved in your area Wildlife Society . . . . ☐

964. Join fellow believers at a religious organization . . . . . . ☐

965. When the ground is covered with snow, be a good duck and feed the birds . . . . ☐

966. March off to an American Legion function . . . . ☐

967. Attend the Democratic convention . . . . ☐

968. Attend the Republican convention . . . . ☐

969. Join a social club together to make new friends . . . . . . ☐

970. Express yourselves by taking part in a march . . . . ☐

971. Zoom off to a Star Trek convention . . . . ☐

IT'S SHOW TIME

972. Watch Saturday morning cartoons
and share a box of doughnuts . . . . ☐

973. Talk about your favorite television shows and
make plans to watch one in the near future . . . . ☐

974. Audition together for a bit part in a movie . . . . ☐

975. Enjoy the *Cosby* show . . . . ☐

976. Tour a local television station . . . . ☐

977. Attend a high school play . . . . ☐

978. Check out the new videos on VH1 . . . . ☐

979. Spend the afternoon hooking up your new VCR . . . . . . ☐

980. Sneak wine coolers into a movie theater . . . . ☐

981. Stay at home for *Saturday Night Live* . . . . ☐

982. For a change, attend a variety show . . . . ☐

983. Slide on down to an ice show . . . . ☐

984. Critique the season's new television shows . . . . ☐

985. Watch a street magician perform . . . . ☐

986. Attend a motion picture premiere . . . . ☐

987. Chuckle with *Cheers* on Thursday night . . . . ☐

988. Avoid having a dog day afternoon
by attending a dog show . . . . ☐

989. Host a dress rehearsal party . . . . ☐

990. Follow the trials and tribulations of *LA Law* . . . . ☐

991. Go to a ballet recital . . . . ☐

992. Pause for a minute to view a puppet show at the mall . . . ☐

993. Catch a special event on closed circuit television . . . . . . ☐

994. Hurry home to watch *Love Connection* . . . . ☐

995. Gather with friends to cheer for your team
at a bar with a big screen television . . . . ☐

996. Entertain yourselves with HBO . . . . ☐

997. View a one act play . . . . ☐

998. Listen to a motion picture soundtrack . . . . ☐

999. Stay up late to watch David Letterman . . . . ☐

1000. Discover future stars at a talent show . . . . ☐

1001. Browse through a baseball card show . . . . ☐

1002. Sneak away to a matinee . . . . ☐

1003. Rock to MTV . . . . ☐

1004. Shop for knick-knacks at a craft show . . . . ☐

1005. Watch the taping of a television program . . . . ☐

1006. Enjoy yourselves at a comedy club . . . . ☐

1007. Take the time to stop and listen to a street musician . . . . ☐

1008. Keep up with *Thirtysomething* . . . . ☐

1009. For a long date, watch the Academy Awards . . . . ☐

DATING FACT

Most men are flattered when they are asked out.

AROUND THE TOWN

1010. Have a car phone date when you
are both driving home from work . . . . ☐

1011. Go bric a brac hunting at out of the way shops . . . . . . ☐

1012. Take a harbor tour . . . . ☐

1013. Enjoy a picnic at a scenic spot
inside a chauffeured limousine . . . . ☐

1014. Go on a scavenger hunt . . . . ☐

1015. Take a taxi around your city to see the sights . . . . ☐

1016. Ride a double-decker bus . . . . ☐

1017. Put a note in two balloons to see see which one goes
the farthest (the loser buys lunch when the results land) . . ☐

1018. Crash a wedding reception . . . . ☐

1019. Spend a summer's night cruising . . . . ☐

1020. Enjoy the coziness of a corner tavern . . . . ☐

1021. Pitch in and help with the chore of
packing and moving to a new place . . . . ☐

1022. Shop street vendors for bargains . . . . ☐

1023. Go out to a special restaurant to celebrate your raise . . . . ☐

1024. Enjoy a ride in a convertible on a beautiful spring day . . . ☐

1025. Tour a historical building . . . . ☐

1026. Shop the downtown area of your city . . . . ☐

1027. Enjoy a meal at an outdoor cafe on a nice evening . . . . . ☐

1028. View the city lights at night from a skyscraper . . . . ☐

1029. Have dinner at a cafeteria . . . . ☐

CASH OR CHARGE?

1030. Go on a wild, carefree shopping spree . . . . ☐

1031. Thumb through a Spiegel catalog
and share your likes and dislikes . . . . ☐

1032. Hunt for great buys at an outlet mall . . . . ☐

1033. Buy a "Our first Christmas together" ornament . . . . ☐

1034. When you need a unique gift, shop at a novelty store . . . ☐

1035. Sort through the trash and treasures at a flea market . . . ☐

1036. Attend an antique show and be amazed by the prices . . . ☐

1037. Browse a charity shop . . . . ☐

1038. Join in the excitement by placing a bid at an auction . . . . ☐

1039. Try the horseman's favorite stop, go to a tack shop . . . . ☐

1040. Shape up and shop for fitness equipment . . . . ☐

1041. Buy great mementos at a souvenir shop . . . . ☐

1042. Daydream on a winter day at a boat dealership . . . . . . ☐

WHY NOT TRY

1043. Forget your troubles in a jacuzzi for two . . . . ☐

1044. Get in the spirit and make Christmas decorations . . . . . ☐

1045. Host a Friday the 13th party . . . . ☐

1046. Experience the down to earth fun of a mud drag . . . . . ☐

1047. Use apples and oranges to learn how to juggle . . . . . . ☐

1048. Bury your own time capsule of
mementos of your relationship . . . . ☐

1049. Start a baseball card collection . . . . ☐

1050. Take a busman's holiday . . . . ☐

1051. Hoof it to a horse auction . . . . ☐

1052. Waterpaint together . . . . ☐

1053. Don't just complain about your city,
write a letter to the mayor . . . . ☐

1054. Take off and fly remote controlled
planes on a pretty afternoon . . . . ☐

1055. Loosen up with Tai Chi Chaun . . . . ☐

1056. Watch a television crusade . . . . ☐

1057. Meet your friends at a dive bar . . . . ☐

1058. Try your luck and enter a contest . . . . ☐

1059. You won't regret it if you play the game of Sorry . . . . . ☐

1060. Enjoy a Chinese restaurant . . . . ☐

1061. Browse another city's newspaper to
find something unusual to do . . . . ☐

1062. Join millions of cat lovers, and attend a cat show . . . . . . ☐

1063. Do something silly enough
to get in your local newspaper . . . . ☐

1064. Wrap your fun gifts in the Sunday comics . . . . ☐

1065. Invent something . . . . ☐

1066. Warm up with Irish coffee on a cold evening . . . . ☐

1067. Add to your joint stamp collection . . . . ☐

1068. Try making a cheese fondue on a cold night . . . . ☐

1069. Keep up on local events by attending a public meeting . . . ☐

1070. Fix flapjacks for a Saturday supper . . . . ☐

1071. With the remote control in hand,
channel jump on cable television . . . . ☐

1072. Plan for the future together, buy a savings bond . . . . . . ☐

1073. Procrastinate the day away . . . . ☐

1074. Talk about your favorite sports . . . . ☐

1075. Try the expressive art of folk dancing . . . . ☐

1076. Watch and bid during a television
auction for something for the two of you . . . . ☐

1077. Have your portrait professionally made at a studio . . . . . ☐

1078. View the AIDS quilt . . . . ☐

1079. Spice up your life by planting an herb garden . . . . ☐

1080. Learn to rollerblade . . . . ☐

1081. Play computer games . . . . ☐

1082. Stay in shape during the winter by
jogging on an indoor track . . . . ☐

1083. Watch an obedience trial for dogs . . . . ☐

1084. Listen to country music . . . . ☐

1085. Celebrate Ground Hog Day by checking for his shadow . . ☐

1086. Stop an elevator between floors
and have a picnic for two . . . . ☐

1087. Sit on the dock of the bay . . . . ☐

1088. Buy matching BMWs . . . . ☐

1089. Charter a helicopter . . . . ☐

1090. To find something different to do,
flip through your city's magazine . . . . ☐

1091. Gallop off to a dressage event . . . . ☐

1092. Throw a super bowl party . . . . ☐

1093. Pick out star constellations on a clear winter's night . . . . ☐

1094. Buy copies of this book for all of your friends . . . . ☐

1095. Be a sport and let your date practice their presentation . . . ☐

1096. Enjoy yourselves at a dinner . . . . ☐

1097. Make sugar cookies using fun cookie cutters . . . . ☐

1098. Get back to nature and go mountaineering . . . . ☐

1099. Fly away (pilot's license helpful) . . . . ☐

1100. For a change, go to a coin show . . . . ☐

1101. Bebop around town . . . . ☐

1102. Be adventurous and walk along the cliffs . . . . ☐

1103. On a snowy day, escape to a hothouse . . . . ☐

TERRIFIC IDEAS FOR SMALL OR UNEXPECTED GIFTS

Beach towels	Balloons
Heart shaped boxes	Candy
A special desert	Book
Homemade jam	Stuffed animals
Silver bud vase	Flowers
Music box	Photos of you
Hershey kisses	T-shirts
An engraved gift	CD
Tickets to an event	Cologne
Magazine subscription	Posters
New gadget	A tin of cookies
Wine	Homemade brownies
Monogrammed gym bag	Bookmark
Homegrown veggies	A gift for a pet

SOCIAL LIFE

1104. Start off your weekend at a Friday night cocktail party . . . ☐

1105. Double date . . . . ☐

1106. Celebrate Boss's Day by throwing a small party . . . . . . ☐

1107. Dive into summer by hosting a pool party . . . . ☐

1108. Fellowship at a church supper . . . . ☐

1109. Hobnob together at a black tie reception . . . . ☐

1110. Join in the celebration at a Presentation Ball . . . . ☐

1111. Team up to host a New Year's Day
breakfast for your family . . . . ☐

1112. Rent out a spa for a party . . . . ☐

1113. After playing 18 holes, meet for
lunch at the country club . . . . ☐

1114. Be a sport and suffer through a business dinner . . . . . . ☐

1115. Support a Junior League function . . . . ☐

1116. Go out to dinner with your parents . . . . ☐

1117. Mingle with your friends at a wedding reception . . . . . . ☐

1118. Cover all the bases and throw a World Series party . . . . ☐

1119. Go to a family birthday dinner . . . . ☐

BE PREPARED

1120. Prepare an earthquake survival kit . . . . ☐

1121. Team up to decorate for your party . . . . ☐

1122. Take a first aid class together . . . . ☐

1123. Pack your picnic basket . . . . ☐

1124. Arrange to have Happy Birthday
sung after dinner at the restaurant . . . . ☐

1125. Help prepare the hors d'oeuvres
before your guests arrive . . . . ☐

1126. Enroll in a auto repair class together . . . . ☐

1127. Practice your "Boss, I want a raise" speech . . . . ☐

1128. Check the batteries in your smoke detectors . . . . ☐

1129. Study together . . . . ☐

1130. Read the Sunday ads to plan your bargain shopping . . . . ☐

1131. Assemble a first aid kit . . . . ☐

1132. Don't get all shook up, attend an
earthquake preparedness seminar . . . . ☐

1133. Practice your putting in the living room . . . . ☐

1134. Take a self defense class together . . . . ☐

1135. Learn CPR . . . . ☐

SUITOR'S FAVORITES

1136. Savor the brief moments of a spectacular sunset . . . . . . ☐

1137. Take a walk arm in arm in the falling snow . . . . ☐

1138. Talk the afternoon away at an
enclosed sidewalk cafe on a rainy day . . . . ☐

1139. Share your feelings by writing a love poem together . . . . ☐

1140. Enjoy McDonalds by candlelight
on the living room coffee table . . . . ☐

1141. Watch *Gone With The Wind* . . . . ☐

1142. Share wine from a boda . . . . ☐

1143. Order dinner from an expensive restaurant
in a distant city and have it flown in . . . . ☐

1144. Start your own traditions . . . . ☐

1145. Make plans for future dates together . . . . ☐

1146. Relax with hot buttered rum by a roaring fire . . . . ☐

1147. Unwind to the sounds of Anita Baker . . . . □

1148. Treat yourselves to a catered dinner at home . . . . □

1149. When the power fails... . . . . □

1150. Rendezvous in the bathroom at
a party for a clandestine kiss . . . . □

1151. Host a private girlfriend/boyfriend appreciation party . . . . □

1152. Turn off the world and enjoy each other . . . . □

1153. *Love Story*...read, watch and cry . . . . □

DATING FACT

Time proven advice: you can't judge a book by its cover.

OFF THE BEATEN TRACK

1154. If you love Perry Mason, try the real
thing by observing a trial in progress . . . . □

1155. To get your heart pumping, go through a haunted house . . □

1156. Throw a backwards party, where everyone
comes dressed with their clothes inside out,
walks backwards and speaks in pig latin . . . . □

1157. Meet for breakfast before work . . . . □

1158. Rent a tandem bicycle to go exploring . . . . □

1159. Do doughnuts in a parking lot after a snowfall . . . . . . □

1160. Expand your artistic abilities by
taking a tole painting class . . . . □

1161. Tour a docked ship (you can be
sure that you won't get seasick) . . . . □

1162. Color night out - pick a color, then
choose a restaurant that is decorated in
that color and wear that color and go . . . . ☐

1163. Spend a Saturday afternoon together running errands . . . ☐

1164. Write the governor to express your concerns . . . . ☐

1165. Fall in line and visit a fort . . . . ☐

1166. Discover the underwater world at an aquarium . . . . ☐

1167. For a new twist of dinner and a movie, make
a meal out of the concessions at the theater . . . . ☐

1168. Go to a boxing match . . . . ☐

1169. Get in the spirit and tour a distillery . . . . ☐

1170. A double header date - play two
different sports on one date . . . . ☐

1171. Take part in a political function . . . . ☐

1172. Enjoy a walk along a wharf at sunset . . . . ☐

1173. Go motorcycle riding on the back roads . . . . ☐

1174. To find something out of the
ordinary, browse a museum shop . . . . ☐

1175. Stroll through an open air market . . . . ☐

1176. Host a "come as you are" party . . . . ☐

1177. Shop a wholesale club for some unusual buys . . . . ☐

1178. Make a jack-o-lantern . . . . ☐

1179. For a taste of Mexico, go out for margaritas . . . . ☐

1180. Rendezvous at a park during your
lunch hour for a brown bag meal . . . . ☐

1181. Watch a juggler . . . . ☐

1182. Experience a stockyard auction . . . . □

1183. Treat yourselves to a hibachi meal . . . . □

1184. For an easygoing afternoon, play Yahtzee . . . . □

1185. Launch a pontoon boat party . . . . □

1186. Be patriotic by working at the polls . . . . □

1187. Wander through a Chinese garden . . . . □

1188. Loosen up and enter a limbo contest . . . . □

1189. Enjoy *La Boheme* (opera) . . . . □

1190. Try tobogganing . . . . □

1191. Tone up by pumping iron . . . . □

1192. Discover a secluded beach and
savor life away from civilization . . . . □

1193. Mellow out at a blues bar . . . . □

A WAY TO THE HEART IS THROUGH
THE TUMMY

1194. Enjoy a midnight dinner by candlelight . . . . □

1195. Share red licorice strings at the movies . . . . □

1196. Have a food fight . . . . □

1197. Take a gourmet cooking class together . . . . □

1198. Finger paint with pudding . . . . □

1199. Select choice meat at a butcher
shop for your dinner party . . . . □

1200. Make a meal from vending machines . . . . ☐

1201. Name all of your favorite foods . . . . ☐

1202. Gather nuts in the fall for holiday decorations . . . . ☐

1203. Visit a patisserie and indulge yourselves . . . . ☐

1204. Make a homemade pizza . . . . ☐

1205. Pick blueberries and then bake a pie . . . . ☐

1206. Bake brownies together, then top
with vanilla ice cream, whipped
cream and nuts, and then go hog wild . . . . ☐

1207. Create a three egg omelet masterpiece . . . . ☐

1208. Go on a diet fling - get off
your diet for one fabulous meal . . . . ☐

1209. Spoil yourselves with chocolate
fondue, fresh fruit & champagne . . . . ☐

1210. Host a backyard barbecue . . . . ☐

1211. Prepare your favorite recipe together . . . . ☐

1212. Treat yourselves to strawberry shortcake . . . . ☐

1213. Devour a box of fudge while watching television . . . . . . ☐

1214. Sample delectables at a food fair . . . . ☐

INSTEAD OF ALWAYS SENDING ROSES

Tulips	Mums
Violets	Silk flowers
Carnations	Chocolate roses
A plant	Miniature rose bush
Fresh floral bouquet	Daisies

THE GREAT OUTDOORS

1215. Relax while watching a sailboat race . . . . ☐

1216. Walk around your neighborhood
to enjoy the Christmas lights . . . . ☐

1217. Marvel at a water show . . . . ☐

1218. Continue the tradition of hiding Easter eggs . . . . ☐

1219. See a summer play at an amphitheater . . . . ☐

1220. Go fly a kite . . . . ☐

1221. Experience a windjammer cruise . . . . ☐

1222. Race to the bottom of a water slide . . . . ☐

1223. Bundle up and go outside to play in the snow . . . . ☐

1224. Enjoy the sunshine while throwing a frisbee in the park . . . ☐

1225. Wash your hair together in the pouring rain . . . . ☐

1226. Build a fabulous sand castle . . . . ☐

1227. Snuggle up next to a campfire on the beach . . . . ☐

1228. Team up to hunt for a four leaf clover . . . . ☐

1229. Spend a day together at a ranch . . . . ☐

1230. Sit on a riverbank and daydream what
your lives will be like ten years from now . . . . ☐

1231. Enjoy a walk in the rain on a summer day . . . . ☐

1232. When all other conversation
fails, talk about the weather . . . . ☐

1233. Join your friends at a volleyball party . . . . ☐

1234. Bury each other in fall leaves . . . . ☐

1235. Support the Audubon Society . . . . ☐

1236. Get up and go, after learning how to water ski . . . . . . ☐

1237. Experience the thrill of inner tubing behind a speedboat . . ☐

1238. Branch out and climb a tree . . . . ☐

1239. Gather flowers from your garden . . . . ☐

1240. Host a BYOF (fireworks) extravaganza
on Uncle Sam's birthday . . . . ☐

1241. Watch a log rolling contest . . . . ☐

1242. Sneak away for a picnic in the middle
of a football field in an empty stadium . . . . ☐

1243. Wander through a nearby state park . . . . ☐

BE TEAM PLAYERS

1244. On the evening of April 14th, help prepare tax forms . . . . ☐

1245. Get away for a Saturday canoe trip . . . . ☐

1246. Share your class notes . . . . ☐

1247. Coach a little league team together . . . . ☐

1248. Pick out and address Christmas cards . . . . ☐

1249. Caddie for your date at a golf tournament . . . . ☐

1250. Make a "create as you go" spaghetti sauce . . . . ☐

1251. Help him decorate his office . . . . ☐

1252. Dress alike for the day . . . . ☐

1253. Improve your health by starting a
cholesterol lowering diet together . . . . ☐

1254. Taxi your date while their car is in the shop . . . . □

1255. Help with the dishes . . . . □

1256. If you are tired of bouncing all over town,
stay at home to balance your checkbooks . . . . □

1257. Team up to aid the Red Cross during a disaster . . . . . . □

1258. Sneak away for the day together after calling in sick . . . . □

1259. Design a couples' Halloween
costume for the two of you . . . . □

1260. Try a merger - invest in a penny stock together . . . . □

1261. Help prepare a resume . . . . □

1262. Have a rummage sale together and use the proceeds
to splurge for an expensive night out on the town . . . . . . □

1263. Spend the day parasailing . . . . □

1264. Cheer from the sidelines for your date . . . . □

1265. Help him shop for clothes . . . . □

PLACES TO GO - THINGS TO DO

1266. Browse through an art gallery . . . . □

1267. Enjoy a casual supper at a friend's place . . . . □

1268. For a day of adventure, go yachting . . . . □

1269. Tour a winery . . . . □

1270. Pick out a nearby unknown town on
the map and spend the day exploring . . . . □

1271. Get lost in a maze . . . . □

1272. Experience a Mexican fiesta . . . . □

1273. Join the old gang during a homecoming weekend . . . . . □

1274. Meet for a Sunday brunch . . . . □

1275. Go foot stomping at a blue grass festival . . . . □

1276. Make an extravagant purchase together . . . . □

1277. Have dinner at a diner . . . . □

1278. Revive your school spirit at an alumni function . . . . . . □

1279. Treat yourselves to a gourmet picnic . . . . □

1280. Avoid salesmen by Sunday afternoon car shopping . . . . □

1281. Check out an expo . . . . □

1282. Armed with credit cards, go shopping together . . . . . . □

1283. Drift on down to a flatboat race . . . . □

1284. Check out a 4-H Club event . . . . □

1285. Accompany your date to a school function . . . . □

1286. Warm up while shopping at a woolen mill . . . . □

1287. Dine at a grill . . . . □

1288. Celebrate with your friends at their wedding . . . . □

---

*One word frees us of all the weight and
pain of life: that word is love.*
Sophocles

*The cautious suitor who stays on the fence
too long usually ends up getting the gate.*
Anonymous

BLAST FROM THE PAST

1289. Read Shakespeare . . . . □

1290. Delight in a Vaudeville show . . . . □

1291. Reminisce about your past dates together . . . . □

1292. Tour an abandoned mine to search for treasures . . . . . . □

1293. Share childhood memories with each other . . . . □

1294. Hula hoop again . . . . □

1295. Listen to *Mystery Theater* on the radio . . . . □

1296. Explore a ruin . . . . □

1297. Restore an antique car together . . . . □

1298. Relax on a day long steamship ride . . . . □

1299. Enjoy the ambience of a century old bar . . . . □

1300. Go fossil hunting . . . . □

1301. Dress the part and go to a sock hop . . . . □

1302. Share the scale of a weight and fortune machine . . . . . . □

1303. Browse an antique auction . . . . □

1304. Entertain together with an afternoon tea party . . . . . . □

1305. Visit a historic battlefield . . . . □

1306. Journey to a medieval banquet . . . . □

1307. Lift off from your regular routine
      by launching a model rocket . . . . □

1308. Try doing the polka . . . . □

1309. Hunt for treasures at a sports memorabilia auction . . . . . □

1310. Experience a relaxing scenic train ride . . . . ☐

1311. Participate in an archaeological dig . . . . ☐

1312. Share some laughs while looking
through your baby pictures . . . . ☐

1313. Hang out and feel groovy at a 60's bar . . . . ☐

1314. Go touring in an antique car . . . . ☐

WHAT ROMANCE IS ALL ABOUT

1315. Dance the night away . . . . ☐

1316. Enjoy a long walk together at sunset . . . . ☐

1317. Dim the lights and listen to Luther Vandross . . . . ☐

1318. Kiss hello every time that you see each other . . . . . . ☐

1319. Discover the language of love,
take a poetry class together . . . . ☐

1320. Leave the party early so the two
of you can spend some time alone . . . . ☐

1321. Bring her flowers and candy . . . . ☐

1322. Get away for a romantic picnic for two . . . . ☐

1323. Charm the socks off each other . . . . ☐

1324. Instead of a blockbuster, go to
an epic romantic love story . . . . ☐

1325. Watch the submarine races . . . . ☐

1326. Dance the tango, the most romantic dance . . . . ☐

1327. Discover "your" restaurant . . . . ☐

1328. Celebrate your relationship with an elegant
dinner using fine china and crystal . . . . ☐

1329. Sit back and watch the fog roll in over the lake . . . . . . ☐

1330. Take a quiet moonlit walk . . . . ☐

1331. Share an elegant dinner aboard
your yacht (a rented row boat will do) . . . . ☐

TRIED & TRUE

1332. Stay at home and order a Domino's Pizza . . . . ☐

1333. Go to a concert . . . . ☐

1334. If you need a break, shoot pool . . . . ☐

1335. Support your local Civic Theater . . . . ☐

1336. Tell your date about your day at work . . . . ☐

1337. Go sight seeing on a Sunday afternoon . . . . ☐

1338. Listen to the Beatles . . . . ☐

1339. See a movie (a great first date) . . . . ☐

1340. Shop in a department store . . . . ☐

1341. Enjoy dinner at a steak house . . . . ☐

1342. Spend a day together at the mall . . . . ☐

1343. Go out for pizza . . . . ☐

1344. Watch one of the all time favorites, *The Wizzard of Oz* . . . ☐

1345. Take time out of your busy day to meet for lunch . . . . . . ☐

1346. Share all of your jokes . . . . ☐

1347. Prepare a home cooked meal . . . . ☐

1348. Follow the antics of Charlie Brown,
Snoopy and the gang . . . . ☐

1349. Attend a Good Friday service . . . . ☐

1350. Browse a pet store . . . . ☐

1351. Celebrate the birds returning in the
spring with a picnic in the park . . . . ☐

1352. Help her to make decisions when shopping for clothing . . ☐

TOWARDS A BETTER RELATIONSHIP

Maintain open communication

Use tact

Make a list of areas to improve upon
and work on those together

Set up a specific time to discuss problems

Remember that you don't always have to
agree - you can agree to disagree

Have time apart from each other

Keep your friends

Make a list of new activities to do on your dates

Have other interests besides each other

Confront each other when a problem arises,
instead of letting it fester and build

Work at being romantic and thoughtful

WITH A LITTLE HELP FROM YOUR FRIENDS

1353. Challenge other couples to a clabber tournament . . . . . . ☐

1354. Have your friends prepare and serve you two a romantic dinner . . . . ☐

1355. Serve up a volleyball party together . . . . ☐

1356. After the game, meet up with your friends for dinner . . . . ☐

1357. Team up to support a fund raising event . . . . ☐

1358. Group date . . . . ☐

1359. Throw a finals' week party after finals are finally over . . . . ☐

1360. Host a pot luck dinner . . . . ☐

1361. Play peacemaker among other couples having dating problems . . . . ☐

1362. To cut back on expenses, throw a BYOB party . . . . ☐

1363. Have a "mystery date" - a friend makes all of the arrangements . . . . ☐

1364. Shape up together at a Weight Watchers class . . . . ☐

1365. Host a roast . . . . ☐

IT'S MUSIC TO MY EARS

1366. Crank up the Victrola to play your parent's old 78's . . . . . ☐

1367. With your ear plugs ready, attend a rock concert . . . . . . ☐

1368. Enjoy soul music . . . . ☐

1369. While taking a fitness walk through
the park, share a Walkman . . . . ☐

1370. Sing our National Anthem at a ballgame . . . . ☐

1371. Check out a local band . . . . ☐

1372. Go Christmas caroling together . . . . ☐

1373. Listen to new songs on the radio . . . . ☐

1374. Pick out your favorite tunes on a jukebox . . . . ☐

1375. Relax while listening to the
waves crash against the shore . . . . ☐

1376. Share a loveseat to watch the Grammy Awards . . . . . ☐

1377. Sing hymns . . . . ☐

1378. Try yodeling (but not in public) . . . . ☐

1379. Listen to a great pianist perform . . . . ☐

1380. For an evening of perfect harmony,
go to a barbershop quartet concert . . . . ☐

1381. Record your own record . . . . ☐

1382. Prepare for the upcoming winter by
putting up a birdhouse with a feeder . . . . ☐

1383. For a southern flair, enjoy a Dixieland band . . . . ☐

1384. Join in the fun and request your
favorite songs at a piano bar . . . . ☐

1385. Jazz your troubles away . . . . ☐

1386. Pick out "your" song . . . . ☐

1387. Share a blanket while listening
to the rain fall on a tin roof . . . . ☐

LOVE MAKES THE WORLD GO 'ROUND

1388. Enjoy yourselves under a harvest moon . . . . ☐

1389. Share a roll of Life Savers . . . . ☐

1390. Dine at a revolving restaurant and enjoy the view . . . . . . ☐

1391. Visit each other in the hospital . . . . ☐

1392. Take food to a shut-in . . . . ☐

1393. Matchmake your dateless friends . . . . ☐

1394. Join in the celebration at a couples wedding shower . . . . ☐

1395. Tutor a child together . . . . ☐

1396. Ride an old time carrousel . . . . ☐

1397. Go to a Valentine's Day dance with someone special . . . ☐

1398. Visit a picturesque windmill . . . . ☐

1399. Volunteer yourselves to help at an animal shelter . . . . . . ☐

1400. Brighten someone's day by visiting an orphanage . . . . . ☐

1401. Smooch . . . . ☐

1402. Make it a joint effort to cheer up a friend . . . . ☐

1403. Snuggle while riding a Ferris wheel . . . . ☐

PLACES TO MEET MEN

High school tracks	Martial arts classes
Bicycling	Laundromats
Bowling lanes	Work-related meetings
Sporting events	Church
Fitness centers	Sports bars

IF YOU HAVE ALREADY TRIED
THE FIRST 1403...

1404. D^3 date - drinks, dinner & dancing . . . . ☐

1405. Frolic on a playground during your lunch hour . . . . . . ☐

1406. Exchange gifts on New Year's Day . . . . ☐

1407. Listen to Fleetwood Mac . . . . ☐

1408. Host a Sunday supper for your friends . . . . ☐

1409. Improve yourselves by taking a class . . . . ☐

1410. Be a good sport and go along to a doll show . . . . ☐

1411. Pen a limerick together . . . . ☐

1412. Have a doughnut hole breakfast before church . . . . . . ☐

1413. Set up an aquarium in your apartment . . . . ☐

1414. Trade baseball cards . . . . ☐

1415. Write an appreciation letter to your city council . . . . . . ☐

1416. Play Chinese checkers on a cold night . . . . ☐

1417. For an unusual outing, try a visit to a roadhouse . . . . . ☐

1418. Experiment cooking with a wok . . . . ☐

1419. Browse the classifieds for hidden treasures . . . . ☐

1420. Organize a progressive dinner party . . . . ☐

1421. Watch a western . . . . ☐

1422. Call in your joint pledge to a telethon
and challenge other couples to do the same . . . . ☐

1423. Throw an Alaskan gold rush party . . . . ☐

1424. Make your own Candid Camera show
using your unsuspecting friends . . . . ☐

1425. Talk about your favorite books . . . . ☐

1426. In the name of "love", improve your
game by taking tennis lessons together . . . . ☐

1427. Join a sports club . . . . ☐

1428. Set out to break a *Guinness* record . . . . ☐

1429. Host a New Year's Eve bash . . . . ☐

1430. Celebrate the end of summer by
watching the Labor Day Telethon . . . . ☐

1431. Attend a political debate . . . . ☐

1432. Donate plasma . . . . ☐

1433. Listen to the Barber of Seville (opera) . . . . ☐

1434. Rent out a movie theater for a
private, romantic showing for two . . . . ☐

1435. Exchange your business cards to
impress each other with your title . . . . ☐

1436. Go trailblazing . . . . ☐

1437. Watch the Goodwill Games . . . . ☐

1438. Capture special moments with an instant camera . . . . . . ☐

1439. Celebrate a jubilee . . . . ☐

1440. Try imported ale . . . . ☐

1441. Start a coin collection together . . . . ☐

1442. Kick back and enjoy a foot massage . . . . ☐

YOU'LL FEEL THE EARTH MOVE

1443. Go to a ground breaking ceremony . . . . □

1444. Strengthen your relationship
by attending church together . . . . □

1445. Head to the beach for a day of bodysurfing . . . . □

1446. Host a clam dig . . . . □

1447. Flip over each other on a trampoline . . . . □

1448. Pack a lunch and spend the day 4-wheeling . . . . □

1449. Join other concerned citizens at an Earth Day party . . . . □

1450. Turn off the lights and spend a
summer evening thunderstorm watching . . . . □

1451. For a guaranteed blast, watch a rocket launching . . . . . □

1452. Pick grapes and stomp them . . . . □

1453. Loosen up and do the rumba . . . . □

1454. Watch real life cowboys in action at a rodeo . . . . □

CUPID'S CHOICE

1455. Share a candlelight dinner for two . . . . □

1456. Write your initials in wet cement inside a heart . . . . . . □

1457. Dance the night away cheek to cheek . . . . □

1458. Kiss . . . . □

1459. Celebrate your dating anniversaries . . . . □

1460. For a date that is right on target, try archery . . . . ☐

1461. Fall in love all over again . . . . ☐

1462. Make a toast to each other . . . . ☐

1463. Send a picnic basket to her office with a note directing
her to bring it to a romantic spot for a wonderful time . . . . ☐

1464. Bring your date a chocolate rose . . . . ☐

1465. Hold hands during a scary movie . . . . ☐

1466. Sit next to a roaring fire and
compose love letters to each other . . . . ☐

1467. Share a tin of heart shaped cookies . . . . ☐

1468. While at the mall, split up for fifteen minutes
to buy each other a fun five dollar gift . . . . ☐

1469. Enjoy the beauty of a sunset picnic . . . . ☐

1470. Make Valentine's Day special by
celebrating by yourselves . . . . ☐

HIGH TECH ROMANCE

Leave a romantic message on the answering machine

Video tape a special message

Fax a love letter

Make a cassette of your favorite songs

Link-up your computers

Video tape part of your time together

Make a computer print out of all the things
that you like about each other

WE ALL HAVE TO
EAT SOMETIME

1471. Leave out milk and cookies for Santa Claus . . . . ☐

1472. Try an oyster bar . . . . ☐

1473. Fix a junk food feast . . . . ☐

1474. Prepare a vegetarian meal . . . . ☐

1475. When your luncheon plans
flounder, have your own fish fry . . . . ☐

1476. Grocery shop together . . . . ☐

1477. Take off to have dinner at an airport bistro . . . . ☐

1478. For a little variety when dining out,
try samples of each other's meal . . . . ☐

1479. Pig out at a pig roast . . . . ☐

1480. Feast on a fabulous steak dinner
at a "grill your own" restaurant . . . . ☐

1481. Take a cooking class together . . . . ☐

1482. Spell out a special message in your Alphabet soup . . . . ☐

1483. Pick up Chinese food to go . . . . ☐

1484. After a wonderful home cooked meal, go out for dessert . . ☐

1485. Dine at a seafood restaurant . . . . ☐

1486. For a change from burgers and
fries, shop at a health food store . . . . ☐

1487. Make a feast out of "peel your own" shrimp . . . . ☐

DON'T KNOCK IT UNTIL YOU HAVE TRIED IT

1488. Don't be a dead fish, try a sushi bar . . . . ☐

1489. For happy feet, get a pedicure for two . . . . ☐

1490. Learn to hang glide . . . . ☐

1491. Celebrate Victoria Day . . . . ☐

1492. Don't just get mad, express
yourselves by writing to your senators . . . . ☐

1493. Rent a hearse to go to a Halloween party in style . . . . . ☐

1494. Walk along the beach on a winter day . . . . ☐

1495. Play spades . . . . ☐

1496. Browse a hobby shop to discover a shared interest . . . . . ☐

1497. Collect matchbooks from all of the
places that you have been together . . . . ☐

1498. Watch an ice hockey game . . . . ☐

1499. Relax yourselves in a sauna . . . . ☐

1500. Give each other a haircut . . . . ☐

1501. Play black jack, the loser buys lunch . . . . ☐

1502. Explore an oriental food mart . . . . ☐

1503. Dive into an aquatic work out, play water polo . . . . . . ☐

1504. Team up to devise that long overdue budget . . . . ☐

1505. For a hot date, follow a fire truck . . . . ☐

1506. Eat with chopsticks . . . . ☐

1507. Use your artistic abilities while ice sculpting . . . . ☐

1508. Wash your cars in the pouring rain . . . . ☐

1509. Start the day off with a breakfast picnic . . . . ☐

1510. Work on a telethon together . . . . ☐

1511. Make Shakespeare proud by
hosting an Elizabethan party . . . . ☐

1512. Be adventurous and try abseiling . . . . ☐

1513. Go to a smorgasbord and make
little piggies out of yourselves . . . . ☐

1514. Head to the high seas for a day of dolphin watching . . . . ☐

1515. Tread lightly while sharing your political views . . . . . . ☐

1516. Infiltrate an army-navy surplus store . . . . ☐

1517. Try jet skiing . . . . ☐

1518. Attempt to brew homemade beer . . . . ☐

1519. Celebrate Guy Fawkes Day . . . . ☐

1520. Meet for a tavern lunch on a Saturday afternoon . . . . . ☐

1521. Give each other a facial . . . . ☐

1522. While out and about on the town, land at an
airport duty free shop for a major bargain . . . . ☐

1523. Create a masterpiece on canvas . . . . ☐

1524. Get you ears pierced together . . . . ☐

1525. Have a picnic in the bottom of an empty pool . . . . ☐

DATING TIP

The one who does the asking out, does the paying.

OLD FASHIONED FUN

1526. Share a milkshake at a soda fountain . . . . □

1527. Gather seashells by the seashore . . . . □

1528. When you are very hungry, chow down
at a family style restaurant . . . . □

1529. Join in the fun at a church picnic . . . . □

1530. Make Christmas stockings to get ready for Santa . . . . . □

1531. Put on your overalls and go to a barn dance . . . . □

1532. Tell ghost stories on a stormy night . . . . □

1533. Visit in the parlor . . . . □

1534. Feed the ducks in the park . . . . □

1535. Discover treasures in a country store . . . . □

1536. Go swing dancing . . . . □

1537. Spend a rainy afternoon haylofting . . . . □

1538. Watch a classic movie . . . . □

1539. Go ice skating at a local rink . . . . □

1540. Put together a 1000 piece puzzle in one night . . . . . . □

1541. Attend a 4-H fair . . . . □

1542. Play checkers in a country store . . . . □

1543. Play bingo together . . . . □

1544. Warm up to a bonfire on the beach . . . . □

1545. Pop popcorn for an evening in front of the television . . . . □

1546. Enjoy the aroma while baking bread . . . . □

1547. Host a Labor Day picnic . . . . ☐

1548. String cranberries for your Christmas tree . . . . ☐

1549. On a summer's evening, load up the
car and head to a drive-in movie . . . . ☐

1550. Visit with your family . . . . ☐

1551. Listen to Elvis in your blue suede shoes . . . . ☐

1552. Shop for beautiful homemade heirlooms at a quilt show . . ☐

1553. Bake Valentine cookies . . . . ☐

1554. See if time flies, when you're having
fun, by telling time on a sundial . . . . ☐

1555. Pick apples . . . . ☐

1556. Compete at a friendly game of pinball . . . . ☐

1557. Swivel the afternoon away while eating at the counter . . . ☐

1558. Go to a tractor pull . . . . ☐

1559. Share cotton candy . . . . ☐

1560. Shop for garden fresh goodies at a farmer's market . . . . ☐

1561. Win a goldfish at the fair . . . . ☐

1562. Be pirates and go on a treasure hunt . . . . ☐

1563. Celebrate the season at a Christmas party . . . . ☐

1564. Shop at a Five & Dime store . . . . ☐

1565. Watch a Thanksgiving Day parade . . . . ☐

1566. After checking each one, select
and chop down a Christmas tree . . . . ☐

1567. Enjoy a meal at a country inn . . . . ☐

1568. Try candle making together . . . . ☐

1569. Go to a barbecue . . . . ☐

1570. Share an ice cold watermelon on a hot summer day . . . . ☐

> *Courtship consists in a number of quiet*
> *attentions, not so pointed as to alarm,*
> *nor so vague as not to be understood.*
> Sterne

MAKING GREAT MEMORIES

1571. Play hooky together . . . . ☐

1572. Look through your high school
yearbook and share memories . . . . ☐

1573. Host a Great Gatsby party . . . . ☐

1574. Get lost on purpose and enjoy the adventure . . . . ☐

1575. Celebrate a church homecoming . . . . ☐

1576. Rent a video camera to record
the highlights of your date . . . . ☐

1577. Work together in a darkroom and see what develops . . . . ☐

1578. Visit your alma mater . . . . ☐

1579. Start a scrapbook of your dates together . . . . ☐

1580. Have your caricatures sketched by a street artist . . . . . . ☐

1581. Share the excitement of your first kiss . . . . ☐

1582. Invent your own holiday . . . . ☐

1583. Bake Christmas goodies together to give as gifts . . . . . . ☐

1584. Visit with your grandparents . . . . ☐

1585. Team up to play an elaborate
practical joke on a good natured friend . . . . ☐

1586. Worship together at a Christmas Eve service . . . . ☐

1587. Dress up in costumes to have your
picture taken at a custom photo booth . . . . ☐

1588. Stroll through your old neighborhood together . . . . . . ☐

TO HOBNOB

1589. Meet for happy hour with friends . . . . ☐

1590. Enjoy yourselves while dining at the club . . . . ☐

1591. Rent an expensive sports car
and drive by your friends' houses . . . . ☐

1592. Start a fan club together . . . . ☐

1593. Hang out at the Student Union with
the gang on a Saturday afternoon . . . . ☐

1594. Enjoy a fine meal at a yacht club . . . . ☐

1595. Go to a chili dinner at school . . . . ☐

1596. Rent an RV to tailgate in style . . . . ☐

1597. Write to your favorite celebrity . . . . ☐

1598. Host a wine and cheese party . . . . ☐

1599. Hoof it to an Elk's Club dance . . . . ☐

1600. Meet up with your co-workers for an evening . . . . ☐

1601. Start the day off with a champagne breakfast . . . . ☐

> **THE CASE AGAINST SINGLE'S BARS**
>
> Often too loud to talk
>
> Lying abounds
>
> Many are looking for a one night stand
>
> Not everyone is single
>
> Can be expensive
>
> Peer pressure
>
> A lot of game playing
>
> "Plastic" people
>
> Can be very depressing
>
> Emotionally draining if done frequently

PROVEN WINNERS

1602. Make a late night junk food run . . . . ☐

1603. Mingle with your old friends
and make new ones at a party . . . . ☐

1604. Treat your date to their favorite dinner . . . . ☐

1605. Observe Memorial Day together by laying wreaths on the
graves of your loved ones and sharing fond memories . . . ☐

1606. Kick back and listen to Phil Collins . . . . ☐

1607. Enjoy a romantic sunrise walk on the beach . . . . ☐

1608. Be chocoholics together . . . . ☐

1609. Buy a lottery ticket and dream . . . . ☐

1610. Join in the excitement at a professional football game . . . ☐

1611. Try a basic date - go out to eat . . . . ☐

1612. Celebrate a red letter day . . . . ☐

1613. Break out of your winter doldrums
by going to a Super Bowl party . . . . ☐

1614. Share M&Ms . . . . ☐

1615. Putter around all day long together . . . . ☐

1616. Read *Garfield* . . . . ☐

1617. After a deep freeze, go ice skating outdoors . . . . ☐

1618. Throw a gala party . . . . ☐

1619. Go out for a steak dinner . . . . ☐

1620. Host a Halloween party . . . . ☐

1621. Attempt to win a prize at the carnival . . . . ☐

1622. Videotape your date playing sports . . . . ☐

1623. Share Oreo cookies and milk after a long day . . . . . . ☐

1624. Discuss current events . . . . ☐

1625. Watch the Westminster Dog Show . . . . ☐

1626. Take it easy while celebrating Labor Day . . . . ☐

1627. Volunteer to be the designated driver . . . . ☐

1628. Fix a snack together . . . . ☐

1629. Spend the day at a theme park . . . . ☐

1630. View a touring exhibit at the museum . . . . ☐

1631. Join in the excitement of a ticker-tape parade . . . . . . ☐

1632. Watch *The Tonight Show* . . . . ☐

1633. Share your best travel stories . . . . ☐

1634. Enjoy a quick meal at a fast food restaurant . . . . ☐

1635. Read the Sunday paper on a lazy afternoon . . . . ☐

1636. Learn to ballroom dance . . . . ☐

1637. Bake Toll House cookies . . . . ☐

1638. Celebrate July 4th by creating
some fireworks of your own . . . . ☐

1639. Share expenses on a dutch treat date . . . . ☐

1640. Go nightclubing . . . . ☐

1641. Make chili on a cold night . . . . ☐

1642. Amuse yourselves at an amusement park . . . . ☐

1643. Invite your friends over for a quiet evening . . . . ☐

1644. Relax at the beach . . . . ☐

1645. Treat yourselves to a Dairy Queen Blizzard . . . . ☐

1646. Watch a professional tennis match . . . . ☐

1647. Make tacos for your pals . . . . ☐

1648. Share your daily events . . . . ☐

1649. Enjoy a musical . . . . ☐

1650. Join the crowd at a New Year's Eve party . . . . ☐

LEARNING CAN BE FUN

1651. Spend a quiet afternoon together in the library . . . . . . ☐

1652. Play along with a television game show . . . . ☐

1653. Cure your "search & peck" method
by taking a typing class together . . . . ☐

95

1654. Share your expertise by tutoring each other . . . . ☐

1655. Grab a blanket and study on the lawn . . . . ☐

1656. Teach each other the intricacies of your favorite sport . . . ☐

1657. Learn about yourselves at a handwriting analyst . . . . . ☐

1658. Get the facts straight by reading the *Almanac* together . . . ☐

1659. Tackle a project from a "how to" book . . . . ☐

1660. Get in the swing of things by taking golf lessons . . . . . . ☐

1661. Volunteer to teach Vacation Bible School . . . . ☐

1662. Dazzle each other with your knowledge
while playing Trivial Pursuit . . . . ☐

1663. Teach your dog tricks . . . . ☐

1664. Take keyboard lessons together . . . . ☐

1665. Help each other write computer programs . . . . ☐

SHOP 'TILL YOU DROP

1666. Buy decorations the day after Christmas for half price . . . ☐

1667. Hunt for goodies at a church bazaar . . . . ☐

1668. Browse the video store for a movie to rent . . . . ☐

1669. Check out a library book sale . . . . ☐

1670. Go apartment hunting . . . . ☐

1671. The lazy way to shop - thumb
through a Sear's catalog together . . . . ☐

1672. Team up to haggle for the
best price from a street vendor . . . . ☐

96

1673. Search for a good buy at a thrift shop . . . . □

1674. Sort through the junk at a yard sale . . . . □

1675. Go to a pet store to fetch
home unique toys for your pet . . . . □

1676. Browse an L.L. Bean catalog . . . . □

1677. Instead of fighting the mall traffic,
stay at home to shop by phone . . . . □

1678. Help her pick out her perfume . . . . □

1679. Help him pick out his cologne . . . . □

1680. Catch your breath and grab a
bite to eat at the mall food court . . . . □

1681. Clip Sunday coupons for future savings . . . . □

1682. Buy matching Rolex watches . . . . □

1683. Go menu shopping in a restaurant district . . . . □

I'D LIKE FOR YOU TO MEET

1684. Introduce your date to your best friend . . . . □

1685. Collect autographs together . . . . □

1686. Meet for cocktails with a sibling . . . . □

1687. Tell Santa what you want for Christmas . . . . □

1688. Watch an Elvis impersonator . . . . □

1689. Tell humorous family stories . . . . □

1690. Visit a wax museum . . . . □

1691. Meet her sorority sisters . . . . □

97

1692. Meet his fraternity brothers . . . . ☐

1693. Tell tales about your co-workers . . . . ☐

1694. Introduce your boss to your date . . . . ☐

1695. Look through your college yearbook . . . . ☐

1696. Trace your family trees to uncover any nobility . . . . . . ☐

1697. Have your date meet your pet . . . . ☐

1698. Introduce your date to your parents . . . . ☐

1699. Watch a Billy Graham crusade . . . . ☐

1700. Go backstage after a concert . . . . ☐

REASONS FOR YOU TO ENTERTAIN

It is great fun

It can give an occasion a more special feeling

You'll get a return invitation

It could rekindle an old flame or spark a new one

It is a neat way to say thanks for a special night out

People like being invited

It is a way to impress your date

It provides a relaxed atmosphere to
learn more about another person

It is a super way to meet new people

CELEBRATE

1701. Exchange a small gift on St. Nicholas night . . . . ☐

1702. Join in the fun of a couples baby shower . . . . ☐

1703. Observe Martin Luther King Day . . . . ☐

1704. Turn Flag Day into a gala
event by having a huge party . . . . ☐

1705. Attend a Lenten service together . . . . ☐

1706. Go to a July 4th picnic . . . . ☐

1707. Pass out candy cigars after your dog
has puppies or your cat has kittens . . . . ☐

1708. Gather with old friends at a college reunion . . . . ☐

1709. Celebrate Mardi Gras by dressing up in fun costumes
and inviting your pals over for some Cajun food . . . . . . ☐

1710. Enjoy a full moon . . . . ☐

1711. Savor the longest day of the year by
pausing to take stock of your relationship . . . . ☐

1712. Celebrate the Twelve Days of Christmas . . . . ☐

1713. Go out for an anniversary dinner . . . . ☐

1714. Show your pride by flying the flag . . . . ☐

1715. Frolic in the first snowfall of the year . . . . ☐

1716. Toast the Irish with a green beer . . . . ☐

DO YOU ENJOY

1717. Solve the Sunday crossword puzzle together . . . . ☐

1718. Visit a masseuse to unwind . . . . ☐

1719. Share a stromboli . . . . ☐

1720. Watch a barge lock through a dam . . . . ☐

1721. Exercise together to shed a few pounds . . . . ☐

1722. Enjoy cappuccino and conversation . . . . ☐

1723. Try Latin dancing . . . . ☐

1724. Be a sport and watch bowl games
all day long on January 1st . . . . ☐

1725. Make frozen strawberry daiquiris . . . . ☐

1726. Create a work of art with a paint by numbers kit . . . . . ☐

1727. Watch a field hockey game . . . . ☐

1728. Round-up another couple to
shop at a western apparel store . . . . ☐

1729. Be brave and try oysters on the half shell . . . . ☐

1730. Buckle up and take off on a three-wheeler adventure . . . . ☐

1731. Take a walking tour of your city . . . . ☐

1732. Listen to rap music . . . . ☐

1733. Spice up your day by dining at a Mexican restaurant . . . . ☐

1734. Do brass etchings together . . . . ☐

1735. Explore a trade show . . . . ☐

1736. Gather with friends to play Uno . . . . ☐

1737. Create your own special blend of spiced tea . . . . ☐

1738. Lace up your sneakers and play a game of basketball . . . ☐

1739. Rent mopeds for the day . . . . ☐

1740. Discover raggae music . . . . ☐

1741. Visit an orchard . . . . ☐

1742. Attend an awards banquet . . . . ☐

THAT'S SHOW BUSINESS

1743. Watch an Agatha Christie
movie and solve the whodunnit . . . . □

1744. Combine your talents and participate in a talent show . . . □

1745. After dark, watch the stars come out
when hosting a Hollywood party . . . . □

1746. Get on television by doing something outrageous . . . . . □

1747. Experience life at a cabaret . . . . □

1748. After the show, host a cast party . . . . □

1749. Audition for a part in a play together . . . . □

1750. Thumb through *Leonard Maltin's TV Movies &*
Video Guide to find something good to watch . . . . . . □

1751. Be adventurous and try experimental theater . . . . □

1752. Watch a mime artist perform . . . . □

1753. Check out a sneak preview . . . . □

1754. When you can't make it to
Broadway, go see a local play . . . . □

1755. Make a list of your top five movies of all time . . . . □

1756. Enter your four legged buddy in a dog show . . . . □

1757. Participate in community theater together . . . . □

1758. Do your own movie review while
driving home from the cinema . . . . □

1759. Be daring and perform at a Karaoke Club . . . . □

> *Faint heart never won fair lady.*
> Cerrantes

WHEN IN ROME...

New York City

1760. Capture the flavor of the city by street noshing . . . . ☐

1761. Expand your horizons from the
top of the World Trade Center . . . . ☐

1762. Sample the tastes and sounds of Little Italy . . . . ☐

1763. Join trendsetters from all over
he world at Bloomingdale's . . . . ☐

San Francisco

1764. Break out and tour Alcatraz . . . . ☐

1765. Tour Sausalito on a sunny day . . . . ☐

1766. Be awed in the redwood country . . . . ☐

1767. Saunter through Union Square for fabulous shopping . . . ☐

1768. On a Sunday afternoon, join the
crowd at the Golden Gate Park . . . . ☐

St. Louis

1769. Head for "The Hill" for the best
Italian food this side of Rome . . . . ☐

1770. Shop Plaza Frontenac - the midwest's
answer to Rodeo Drive . . . . ☐

1771. Lift your spirits atop the Gateway Arch . . . . ☐

1772. Stroll through the Central West End . . . . ☐

1773. Spend a delightful evening under the stars at the Muny . . ☐

Indianapolis

1774. Feel like a child again as you
tour the Children's Museum . . . . ☐

1775. Enjoy the beauty of Brown County in the fall . . . . ☐

1776. Race to the Indianapolis Motor Speedway for a tour . . . . ☐

Denver

1777. Shop the day away at Larimer Square . . . . ☐

1778. Watch the Broncos play at the
famous Mile High Stadium . . . . ☐

1779. Treat yourselves to one of the free
summertime outdoor symphony concerts . . . . ☐

1780. If you are short on cash, try a visit to the Denver Mint . . . ☐

Dallas

1781. Get on over to the Mesquite Championship Rodeo . . . . . ☐

1782. Fight the massive crowd at the Texas State Fair . . . . . . ☐

1783. Get up early to check out the
goods at the Farmers' Market . . . . ☐

1784. Check out JR's spread at Southfork Ranch . . . . ☐

1785. For an international flavor, try sipping tea while
watching a cricket match at the Dallas Cricket Club . . . . ☐

Nashville

1786. Indulge yourselves with a fabulous
weekend brunch at the Opryland Hotel . . . . ☐

1787. Fiddle the day away on Music Row . . . . ☐

1788. Hop aboard a riverboat replica for
a cruise on the Cumberland River . . . . ☐

1789. Visit the Hermitage to catch a glimpse of the Old South . . ☐

New Orleans

1790. Enjoy the beauty and charm of the
beautiful mansions in the Garden District . . . . ☐

1791. Be entertained with a walk through the French Quarter . . . ☐

1792. If you like big parties, delight
in the festivities of Mardi Gras . . . . ☐

1793. Hunt for hidden artist's treasures along Jackson Square . . ☐

Los Angeles

1794. Watch your step at Mann's Chinese Theater . . . . ☐

1795. Discover all there is to do at Venice Beach . . . . ☐

1796. Get away for the day on Catalina Island . . . . ☐

1797. For a taste of "Olde England" try
the Renaissance Pleasure Faires . . . . ☐

SIGNS THAT YOUR RELATIONSHIP HAS A FUTURE

You enjoy each other

You plan future dates together

You feel mutually committed to the relationship

Your friends consider you a couple

You see each other on a regular basis

You can be yourselves around each other

You look forward to spending time together

WELCOME TO MY ABODE

1798. Show off your new place by hosting
an apartment warming party . . . . ☐

1799. Spend the day on a houseboat . . . . ☐

1800. After a big party, be a good
sport and help clean the carpet . . . . ☐

1801. Team up to tackle the never ending
list of things to fix around the house . . . . ☐

1802. Ask your date to help you bargain
shop for major appliances . . . . ☐

1803. Host an open house during the holidays . . . . ☐

1804. The perfect yuppie date - go condo hunting . . . . ☐

1805. Hang pictures together and get them even for a change . . ☐

1806. Help him decorate his bachelor pad . . . . ☐

1807. Help hang wallpaper . . . . ☐

1808. Build an unusual doghouse - Fido will love this . . . . . . ☐

1809. Enjoy tv dinners in front of the tube . . . . ☐

1810. Go furniture shopping . . . . ☐

1811. Check out several house auctions
for a real estate bargain . . . . ☐

1812. Help rearrange her apartment . . . . ☐

1813. Gather ideas at a Home Show . . . . ☐

1814. Shop for a housewarming gift for a friend . . . . ☐

1815. Put on old clothes to paint your place . . . . ☐

LIFE IN THE FAST LANE

1816. For wintertime excitement, go snowmobiling .... ☐

1817. Learn to ride a skateboard together .... ☐

1818. Rent a golf cart to go for a different kind of Sunday drive .. ☐

1819. Team up in a wheelbarrow race .... ☐

1820. Take driving lessons together .... ☐

1821. Spend the evening at a casino .... ☐

1822. Gallop off to a derby party .... ☐

1823. Enter a three-legged race together at a picnic ...... ☐

1824. Split a split of champagne .... ☐

1825. Hold hands and scream during a roller coaster ride ..... ☐

1826. Get around Chinatown in a rickshaw .... ☐

1827. Don't blink or you might miss the action at a hot rod race .. ☐

1828. Enjoy the fast track while racing slot cars .... ☐

1829. Soak up the rays while you enjoy the day at a regatta ... ☐

1830. Chase down an ice cream truck .... ☐

1831. Gentlemen (and ladies), start your
summer fun at an Indy 500 party .... ☐

1832. Go barhopping together .... ☐

1833. Challenge each other to a pogo stick race .... ☐

1834. Race off to a track meet .... ☐

1835. Try an exhilarating giant slide ride .... ☐

1836. Watch a kayak race .... ☐

1837. Head off into the wild blue yonder
after taking flying lessons together . . . . ☐

1838. Test drive expensive sports cars . . . . ☐

1839. Hold on tight while bobsledding . . . . ☐

1840. Cover your ears during the
thunder of a hydroplane race . . . . ☐

1841. The perfect workout: put on your sweat suit
and running shoes, turn on the television,
sit on the couch and watch the Boston Marathon . . . . . . ☐

1842. Get out of town to watch a cross country road rally . . . . . ☐

1843. Race go karts at an amusement park (the loser
gets a chance to get even at bumper cars) . . . . ☐

WHO SAID THAT THREE IS A CROWD?

1844. Visit a maternity ward together to see a friend's baby . . . ☐

1845. Bring your dog along on a picnic . . . . ☐

1846. Spend a day in the park taking pictures of your pet . . . . . ☐

1847. Drop in on old friends . . . . ☐

1848. Take your cat to the vet . . . . ☐

1849. Make it a fun evening and baby sit together . . . . ☐

1850. Dress your dog in a costume for a special outing . . . . . ☐

1851. Invite a lonely friend along for an evening out . . . . . . ☐

1852. Take your cat with you to a drive-in movie . . . . ☐

1853. Adopt a pet and name it after your date . . . . ☐

1854. Pet sit together . . . . ☐

1855. Invite your minister along to lunch . . . . ☐

1856. Play frisbee with your dog in the park . . . . ☐

EXPRESS YOURSELVES

1857. Give each other a nickname . . . . ☐

1858. Be creative and compose your own song . . . . ☐

1859. Try saying tongue twisters . . . . ☐

1860. Speak in a funny diction for the entire date . . . . ☐

1861. Say grace . . . . ☐

1862. Challenge each other at word games . . . . ☐

1863. Exercise your constitutional rights by voting . . . . ☐

1864. Share part of your diary . . . . ☐

1865. Dress up as your hero and heroine
and go to a costume party . . . . ☐

1866. Fax date . . . . ☐

1867. Amuse yourselves with a game of Scrabble . . . . ☐

1868. Write a letter to Santa . . . . ☐

1869. Read to each other on a lazy spring afternoon . . . . . . ☐

1870. Draw pictures in the sand . . . . ☐

1871. Put a note in a bottle and set it adrift in the sea . . . . . ☐

1872. Take a sculpting class together . . . . ☐

1873. Spend a Saturday morning painting clown faces
at a home for underprivileged children . . . . ☐

1874. Play the Pictionary game . . . . ☐

1875. Volunteer to work together one
night a week at a Crisis Line . . . . ☐

1876. Make a fun prank phone call to a friend . . . . ☐

1877. Speak your mind by writing a letter to the editor . . . . . . ☐

1878. Get published (We did) . . . . ☐

1879. Copyright something (We did that, too) . . . . ☐

1880. Meet for a quick cup of espresso
before work on a winter's morning . . . . ☐

WHAT NOT TO DO ON FIRST DATES

Talk only about yourself

Be late

Compare your present date to past dates

Flirt with others

Tell your life story including private details

Ask your date extremely personal questions

Dress in an inappropriate manner

Expect sex

Be a complainer

Brag

Order food which is difficult to eat

Go somewhere that you aren't comfortable

Make the date too long

Go to a sexually explicit movie

Be "too nice"

LITTLE THINGS MEAN A LOT

1881. Go out on the town to celebrate your new job . . . . ☐

1882. Share a blanket on a cold night at a football game . . . . . ☐

1883. Nurse your date back to health when illness strikes . . . . ☐

1884. Make greeting cards together for your friends . . . . ☐

1885. Eat crow when necessary . . . . ☐

1886. Gift wrap presents by wrapping items in
many boxes tucked inside of each other . . . . ☐

1887. Be a sport and rub Ben Gay on sore aching muscles . . . . ☐

1888. Visit a cemetery together to lend support . . . . ☐

1889. Enjoy being comfortable enough that you
don't feel like you must talk all of the time . . . . ☐

1890. Cure the other of hiccups . . . . ☐

1891. Buy girl scout cookies and share them . . . . ☐

1892. During a tough time, go out of your way to cheer him up . . ☐

1893. Visit a friend in the hospital . . . . ☐

1894. Surprise her with a ride home from work . . . . ☐

1895. Make your date's birthday a festive occasion . . . . ☐

1896. When the flu season hits, chauffeur each other
to the doctor's office when the need arises . . . . ☐

1897. Team up to take your dog to the veterinarian . . . . ☐

1898. Display yellow ribbons to support our overseas troops . . . ☐

1899. Surprise him with a bottle of wine . . . . ☐

2002 Things To Do On A Date

INDEX

To order additional copies of
2002 Things To Do On A Date,
mail $4.95 plus $1.00 for postage to:

**Todd & Tweedworth Publishing
5400 E. Timberwood
Newburgh, IN 47630**

41+65

75290006